Letter Openers

Advertising & Figural

ISBN#: 0-89538-044-7

Published by: L-W Book Sales
P.O. Box 69
Gas City, IN 46933

Please write for our free catalog.

©1996 L-W Book Sales

Printed by IMAGE GRAPHICS, INC., Paducah, Kentucky

Table of Contents

INTRODUCTION

In centuries of old, important papers entrusted to a messenger for delivery would be carefully sealed and stamped with a drop of wax to ensure confidentiality. As the years passed on, a new development made the contents of any note private from eager eyes. This was in the early 18th Century, when the envelope was created merely by folding a piece of stiff paper and applying a small amount of glue to the edges. As convenient as this may have appeared to the countless throngs who have utilized it during the past few centuries, the problem of opening one without damaging the contents proved to be an inconvenience. A simple stroke of a pocket knife or other blade would often work, if done with delicate care as not to slice any important papers within. Many correspondents preferred an easier & safer alternative to keeping a sharpened blade around, especially when large stacks of mail needed tended to in a timely fashion. These needs were met with the introduction of the *letter opener*.

Although rather intrinsically a knife with a duller edge, the letter opener soon developed a reputation of its own. Whereas the knife was a utilitarian device for many tasks, the simple nature and quaintness of a letter opener seemed to appeal to many homes and businesses. A more subtle symbol of the current status quo of the 19th and 20th Centuries, the letter opener evolved from a spartan tool to a delicately crafted piece of kitsch.

The construction of a letter opener can vary as much as the imagination of the crafter. While items of wood, metal, plastic, sterling silver, and ivory are popular, more scarce items have been discovered from such materials as shellacked corncob, colored glass, bone, and mother of pearl. The simple spearhead design has also, in some instances, become a figural piece that is barely recognizable as a letter opener. Sword designs are very common, as are female figurals and other relief forms. Some souvenir openers have an inset lens which, when held to a light source and peered through, depict an image such as a tourist site or people in a variety of poses. A few have been dual-designed to perform a variety of chores, such as doubling as a ruler, can opener, or ink pen, *and* a letter opener.

The advent of mass-produced letter openers provided a new audience for many businesses eager to advertise their products in any way possible. These pieces became available to the American public as free or cheap premiums, usually offered as an incentive with another product or left with a potential customer in lieu of a business card. Many letter openers were also available as one of many pieces in a stationery set, together with items such as an inkwell, paperweight, pen, and calendar.

Letter openers are still available today, yet not as prevalent in years previous. Please be aware, however, that many of the old styles of openers, particularly the brass and cut glass styled items have been found as current reproductions

The legacy of years of letter openers does cast an inviting shadow in the way of collectors. Letter openers are a compelling collectible to many antique enthusiasts. A letter opener collection may spring from items out of an advertising, knife, tool, kitchen, country store, or paper collection. Enterprising shoppers have begun letter opener collections independent from other interests due to the vast numbers of pieces that arise in collector's malls and antique dealer shows and shops. The elegance and variety of forms also add desirability to the keen eye of a collector of relics of the past.

Acknowledgments

L-W Books extends a warm thank you to the following collectors who contributed various pictures and information to help in making this book a success.

Myron Huffman
Hoagland, IN
(219) 639-3290
Antique Advertising,
Breweriana, Soda Fountain, Etc.

Don & Mary Perkins
2317 N. Kessler Blvd.
Indianapolis, IN 46222
Safety & Straight Razors,
Barbershop Memorabilia, Etc.

Wayne Stoops
Ft. Wayne, IN

Pricing Note

The current values in this book should be used only as a guide. They are not intended to set prices, which vary from one region of the country to another. Auction prices as well as dealer prices vary greatly and are affected by condition as well as demand. Neither the publisher nor the contributors assume responsibility for any losses or gains that might be incurred as a result of consulting this guide.

FIGURAL LETTER OPENERS

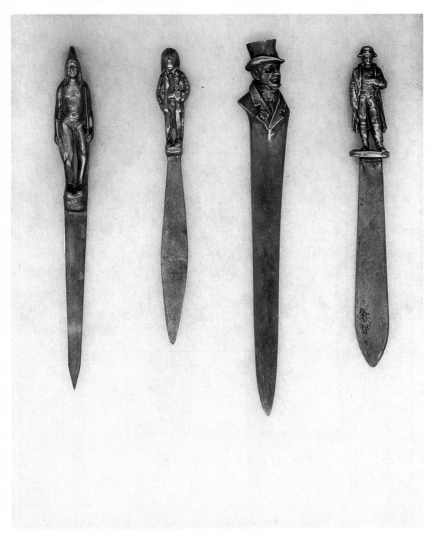

1: Indian Brave; copper; 7 1/4" $50

2: Indian Chief; brass; 6 1/2" $45

3: Charles Dickens; brass; 8" (Made in Austria) $45

4: Napoleon; brass overlay; 7" $40

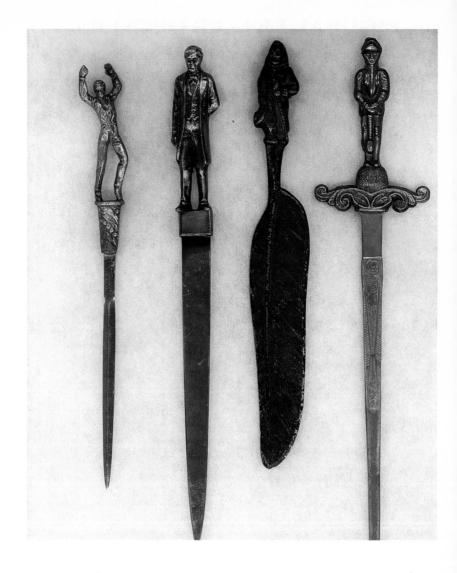

1: Male Dancer; bronze w/ chromed blade; 9" $20

2: Abraham Lincoln; copper; 11" $35

3: Captain John Smith; cast iron; 9 1/4"; ©1957 Va. Metalcrafters;
(inscription "Capt. John Smith, Jamestown 1607- Virginia") $40

4: Armored Knight; bronze w/ steel blade; 12 1/8" $30

1: College Graduate; copper, 7 1/2" $30

2: Egyptian Death Mask; tin & bronze; 5 1/4" $10

3: Indian Chief Profile w/ tassel; copper painted finish;
7 1/2"; (Made in Japan) $10

4: "Tote" Indian Chief; brass; 7"; (the word "TOTE" is imprinted
upon headband of Indian) $15

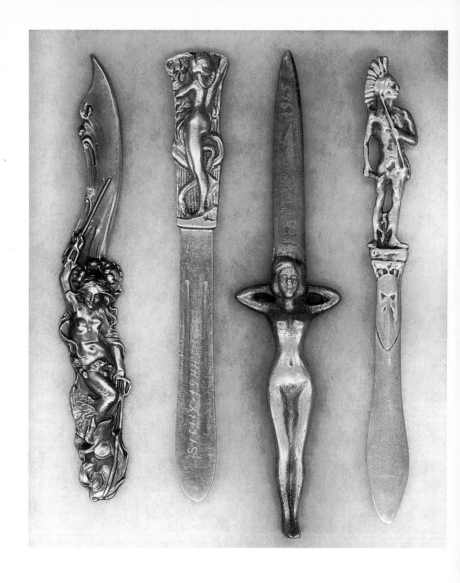

1: Art Nouveau Mermaid; heavy aluminum; 9 1/2";
(Museum of Modern Art piece) $40

2: Art Nouveau Nude; aluminum; 9 1/4"; ("Sicily 1944" stamped
on blade) $25

3: Nudie; aluminum; 10 3/8"; ("Naples 1945" stamped on blade) $30

4: Indian Brave; aluminum; 10"; ("Sicily 1944" stamped on blade) $50

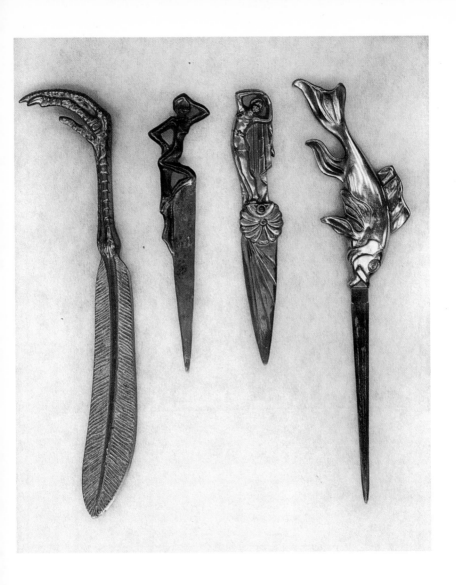

1: Chicken Foot w/ Feather; steel; 9 1/4" $25

2: Deco Nude; bronze w/ green paint; 6"; (Made in Israel) $40

3: Art Nouveau Design; heavy aluminum; 6 1/4"; (with built-in Stanhope viewer) $225

4: Art Nouveau Fish; chromed metal; 9 1/4" ("Chicago 1933" imprinted on blade) $40

1: Bison; copper; 6 1/2"; (front side imprint reads "Pan-American", back side imprint reads "pat. May 14 1901") $125

2: Fish; brass; 7 1/4"; (Made in Israel) $20

3: Parrot; brass; 7 1/2"; (Made in India) $10

4: Alligator; copper coated metal; 7"; (Made in New Orleans) $30

1: Great Horned Owl; cast iron; 8 1/4" $30

2: Sleepy Owl; brass w/ green enamel; 7 1/2"; (Made in Israel) $10

3: Owl Family; bronze; 8 1/2" $30

4: Wide-Eyed Owl; brass; 6"; ("Made in Israel by Nordia") $20

1: Celtic Dragon; brass; 8 1/2" $20

2: Capricorn; brass; 7 1/2" $15

3: Seahorse; copper w/ gilded paint; 9 1/4" $15

4: Horse & Rider; copper w/ gilded paint; 8 1/2" $20

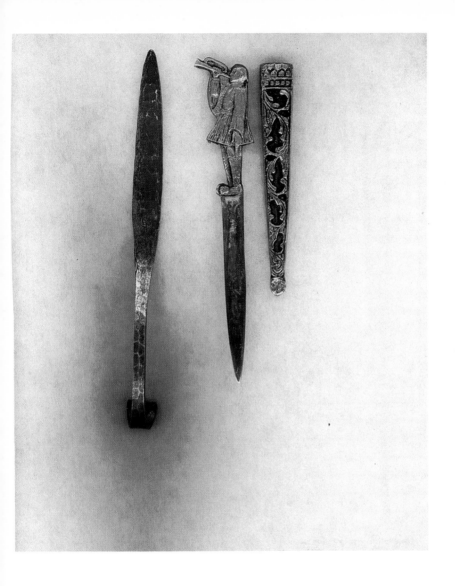

1: Roycroft Letter Opener; hammered aluminum; 8" $100

2: Herald w/ Horn; pewter; 7 3/4"; (complete with pewter sheath) $70

1: Football Design; copper, 9 3/4"; (imprint of "1937" on blade) $25

2: English Fraternity; brass; 9"; (imprint on front reads "TRUSTY SERVANT 1387 WINCHESTER"; imprint on back reads "R<u>d</u> N<u>o</u> 696905 Peerage, England"; also bears "poetic" verse on handle) $35

3: Aeroplane figural; brass; 8 1/4"; (imprint reads "Washington DC) $45

4: Lonely boy; brass; 9"; (Made in Canada) $30

1: Anchor; brass; 9" $15

2: Anchor w/ tassel; copper; 7 3/4" $10

3: Intertwined Hearts; brass; 8 3/4"; (Made in France) $10

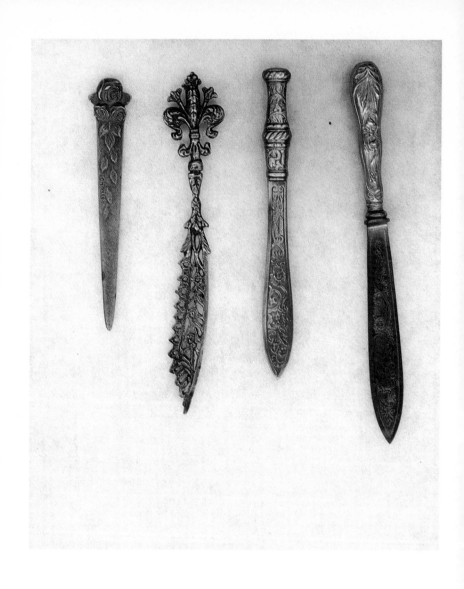

1: Roses; antique brass finish; 5 3/8"; (imprint reads "Charles") $45

2: Intricate Fleurdelis; aluminum; 7 1/4"; (Made in Italy) $20

3: Persian Sword; brass; 6 1/2" $40

4: Floral Design: brass handle & steel blade; 8 1/4" $25

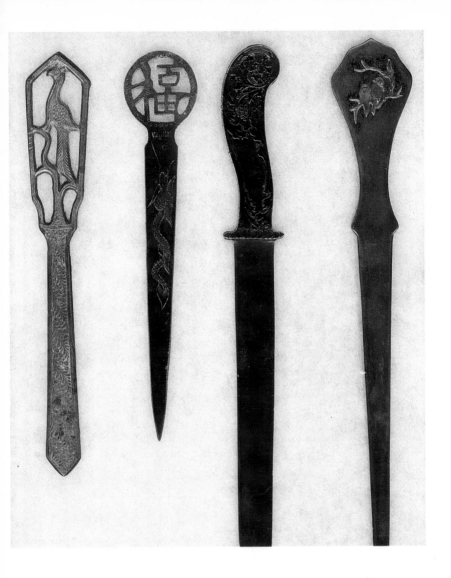

1: Peacock; bronze; 8 3/4" $10

2: Chinese Symbol; brass; 8 1/4"; (Made in China) $10

3: Grapevine Pattern; brass; 11" $20

4: Courting Birds; brass; 11 3/4" $15

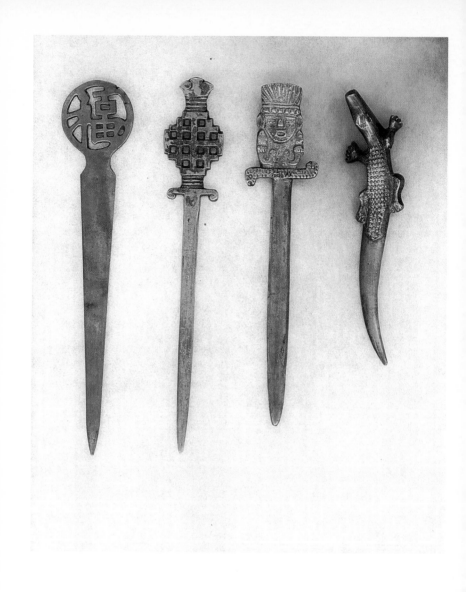

1: Chinese Symbol; brass; 8"; (Made in China) $15

2: Old European Design; brass; 8"; (Made in Israel) $10

3: Incan-style Idol; brass; 7 1/4" $10

4: Alligator; brass; 6"; (Made in China) $10

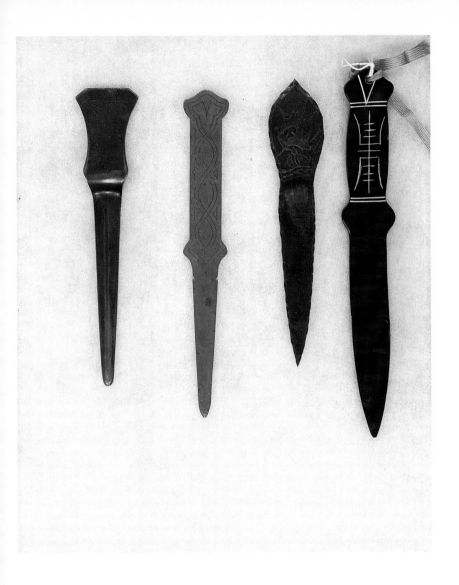

1: Eagle Emblem: copper; 6 1/4" $10

2: Tribal-Style Design; pressed bronze; 6 1/2" $10

3: Sailing Ship; hammered copper; 6" $10

4: Scratch Designs; plastic composite; 8" $5

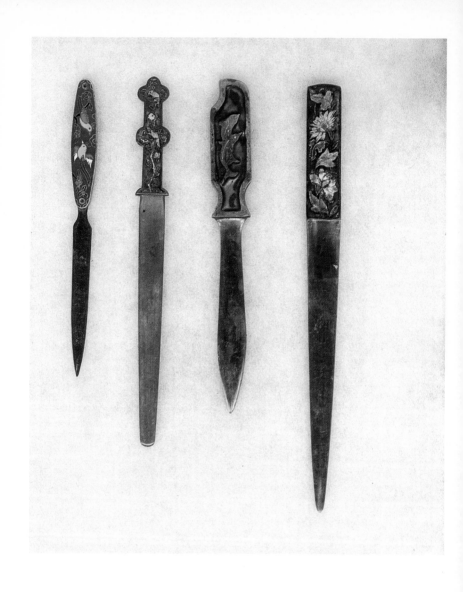

1: Birds of Paradise: painted brass & stainless steel blade; 6 7/8" $10

2: Birds on Branch; painted brass; 7 3/4" $10

3: Dolphins; painted brass; 7" $10

4: Floral Design; painted brass; 9"; (Made in China) $15

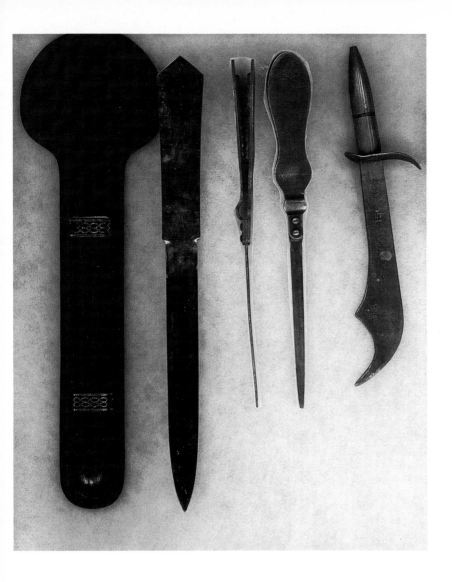

1: Opener and Sheath; black leather sheath and chrome opener; 9 1/2";
(Made in Solingen, Germany) $10

2: (Two views shown) Alligator Clip; copper plated metal; 7 1/2";
 (imprint reads "Pat.July 17 - 06"); (unique handle has serrated teeth
 for removing letter) $45

3: Trench Art; brass; 7 1/4"; (imprint on blade reads "Moluccas
Islands") $15

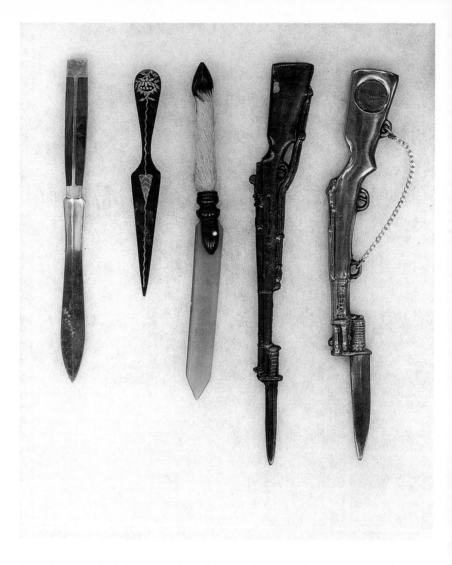

1: Walnut Handled Opener w/ brass blade; 6 3/4"; (Made in Thailand) $10

2: Floral Leaf Pattern; aluminum w/ black enamel finish; 4 3/4" $10

3: Deer Hoof w/ plastic blade; 7" $10

4: M-1 Rifle; aluminumw/ dark enamel; 8 1/2" $15

5: M-1 Rifle; brass w/ medallion on stock; 8 3/4"; (medallion reads "Mt. Vernon, Va") $20

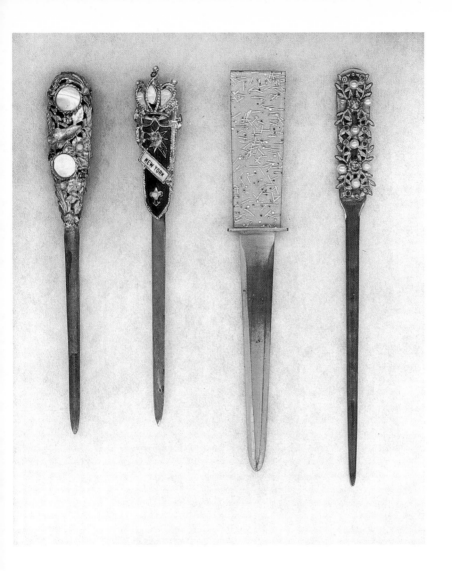

1: Costume Jewelled Leaf Design; stainless steel blade; 7 1/2" $15

2: New York Souvenir w/ costume jewelry; stainless steel blade; 7 1/2" $10

3: Fifties Design; bronze blade; 8 1/2" $20

4: Costume Jewelled Handle: stainless steel blade: 8 3/4" $20

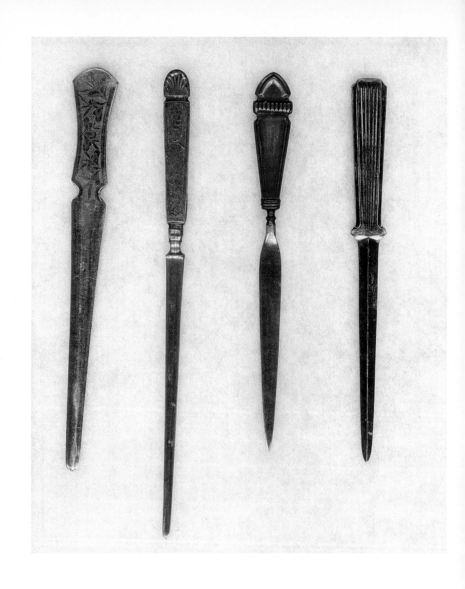

1: Floral Leaf Pattern; stainless steel; 8 1/2"; (Made in China) $10

2: Clamshell & Floral Pattern; stainless steel; 9 3/4" $35

3: Brown Enamelled stainless steel; 8" $10

4: Vertical Design; chromed steel; 8" $10

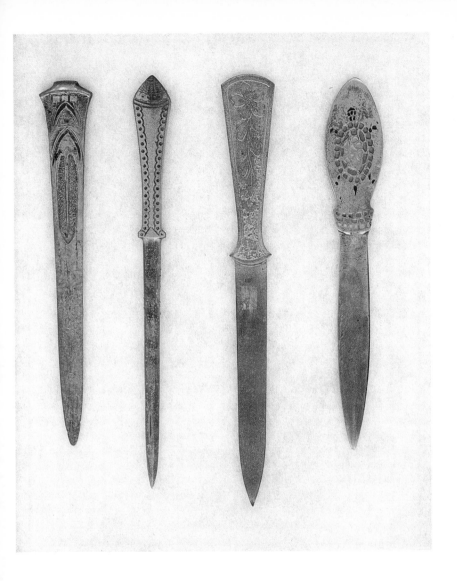

1: Grain Pattern: brass; 7 3/4" $20

2: Dimpled Archaic Design; gilded handle & stainless steel blade; 9") $10

3: Floral Design; gold painted metal; 9" $10

4: Indented Enamel Design; brass; 7 3/4"; (Made in Israel) $10

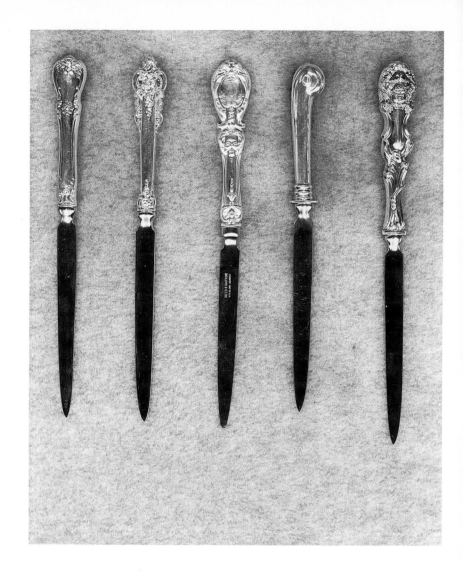

1: *"Old Master"* Design; sterling; 7 5/8"; (Mfg: Towle Silversmiths; ca. 1970-present) $30

2: *"Grand Baroque"* Design; sterling; 7 3/4"; (Mfg: Wallace Silversmiths; ca 1959-1983) $50

3:*"Francis 1st"* Design; sterling; 7 7/8"; (Mfg: Reed & Barton; ca. 1958-present) $30

4:*"Onslow"* Design; sterling; 7 3/8"; (Mfg: Tuttle Sterling Co.; ca. 1992) $30

5: Lion Design; sterling; 8" $30

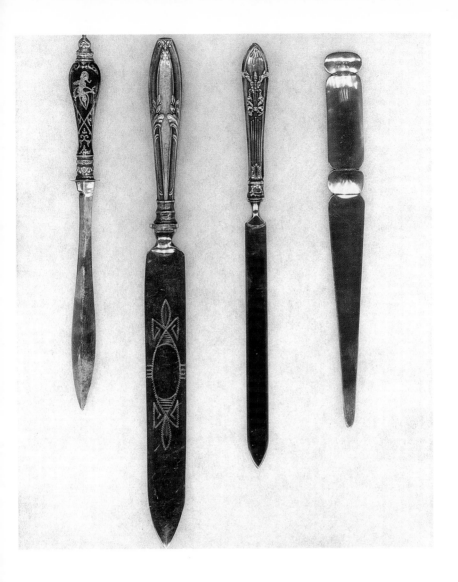

1: Hindu Goddess; sterling; 8" $50

2:Victorian/ Western Design; sterling; 10 7/8"; (marked "MSB") $75

3: Victorian Design; sterling; 9" $50

4: Handmade Design w/ curved handle; sterling; 8"; (marked "Georg
Jensen") $150

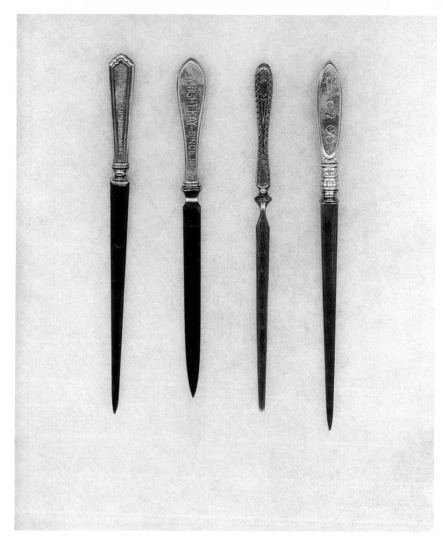

1: "1861- Wright Kay- 1961" Adv.; sterling; 7 5/8"; (Mfg: Webster; ca. 1958) $45

2: "Wright Kay- Since 1861"; sterling; 7 1/4"; (Mfg: Webster; ca. 1958) $60

3: Thin Western Design; silverplated; 7 1/2" $15

4: Monogram Design "VLS"; sterling w/ stainless steel blade; 7 7/8"; (Mfg: Webster; ca. 1958) $45

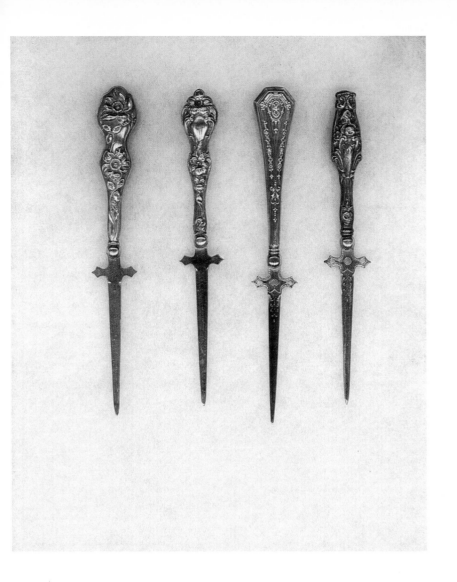

1: Floral French Design; sterling; 7" $50

2: Floral & Vine French Design; sterling; 6 3/4" $50

3: French Design; sterling; 7 1/8" $50

4: Ornate Floral French Style; sterling; 6 5/8" $50

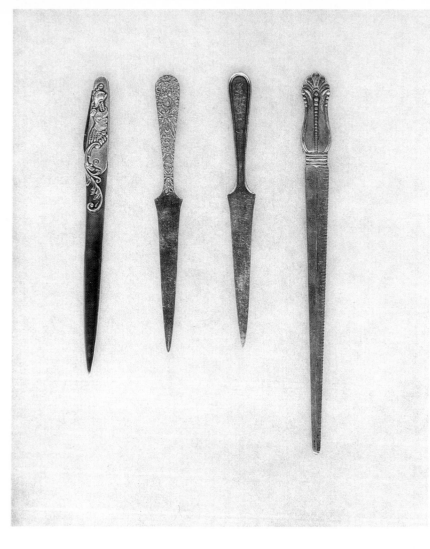

1: Armor Relief Design Opener/ Pocketknife; sterling; 6 3/8";
(Mfg: Hayden Mfg. Co.; ca. 1904-1908) $225

2: Floral Design; sterling; 5 7/8"; (Mfg. S. Kirk & Sons; ca.
1932-1961) $45

3: Monogram Design "CBMcF"; sterling; 5 7/8"; (Mfg: S. Kirk
& Sons; ca. 1927-1961) $40

4: French Design Opener/ Ruler; sterling; 8 1/8"; (Mfg: Frank M.
Whiting Co.; ca. 1896-1940) $145

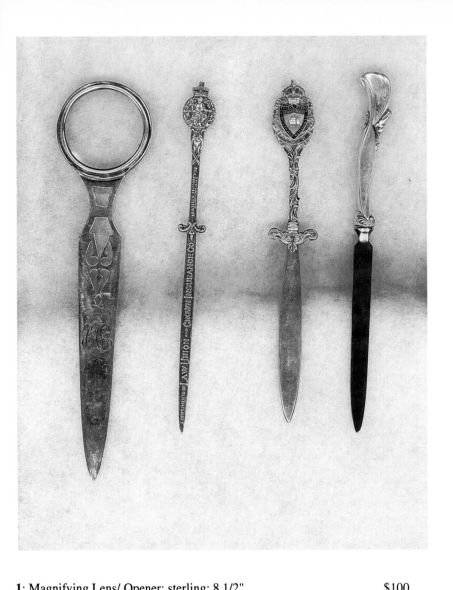

1: Magnifying Lens/ Opener; sterling; 8 1/2" $100

2: "Law Union & Crown Ins. Co." Adv.; sterling; 7 1/2"; (Mfg: Shreve & Co.) $65

3: "Bahamas" Souvenir; sterling; 7 1/4"; (Made in Canada); (Mfg: Baldwin, Miller Co. Inc.; ca. 1912) $35

4: Victorian Design; sterling; 7 1/2"; (Mfg: Wallace Silversmiths) $50

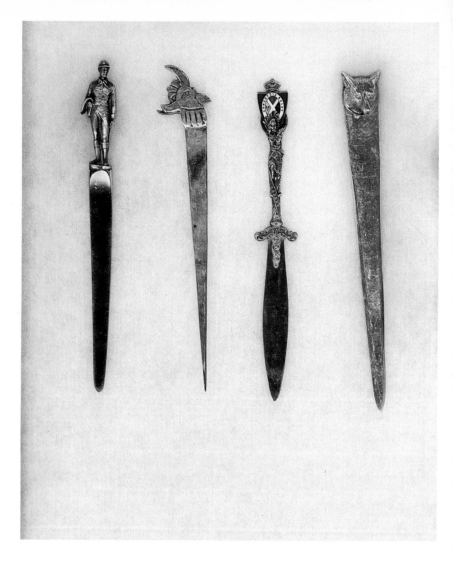

1: Horse Jockey Figural; sterling; 7"; (Mfg: Tiffany & Co.; ca. 1938) $200

2: Mexican Design; sterling; 6 3/4"; (Made in Mexico) $60

3: "Canada" Souvenir; sterling; 6 3/4"; (Mfg: Roden Bros., Ltd; ca. 1904-1915) $30

4: Fox Head Figural; sterling; 7 1/4" $55

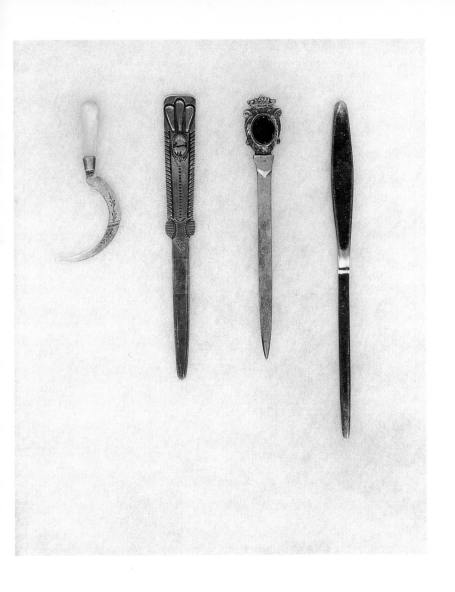

1: Sickle Figural; sterling w/ mother of pearl handle; 3 1/2" $40

2: Inset Stone Design; silverplate; 6" $20

3: Coat of Arms w/ inset stone; sterling; 5 5/8"; (Made in Italy) $40

4: Simple Design; sterling; 7 1/4"; (Mfg: Tuscan Ware) $30

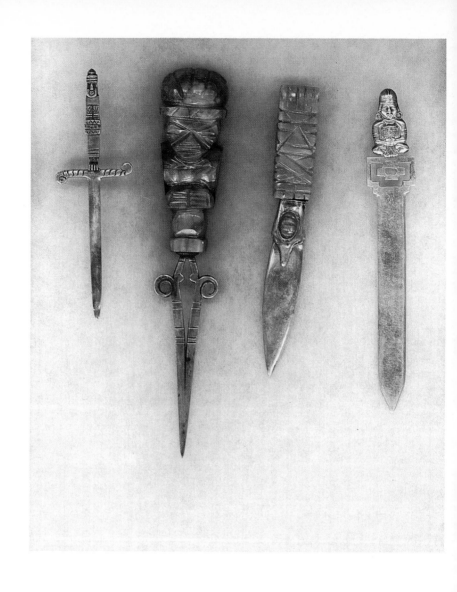

1: Primitive Idol Motif; sterling; 5 1/2" $50

2: Primitive Style Carving; sterling blade; 8 1/4" $50

3: Green Soapstone; sterling blade; 6 1/4"; (Made in Mexico) $50

4: Primitive Idol Motif; sterling; 7"; (imprint reads "Peru 925 FS") $75

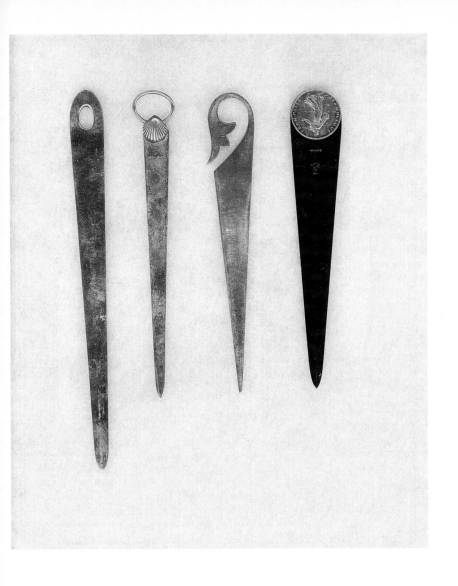

1: Basic Design; sterling; 8 1/4"; (Mfg: Currier & Roby; ca. 1925) $80

2: Sea Shell Design; sterling; 6 1/2"; (Mfg: Juskow) $50

3: American Heritage; sterling; 6 3/8"; (Mfg: Gorham; ca. 1949-1967) $45

4: Inset Franc Design; sterling; 6 3/8"; (Mfg: Dunhill; ca. 1918) $45

1: Bird Figural; bone; 6 1/4" $25

2: Chinese Dragon w/ tassel; bone; 7 1/4" $15

3: Scimitar Design; bone; 6" $20

4: Intricate Design; bone; 7 3/8" $25

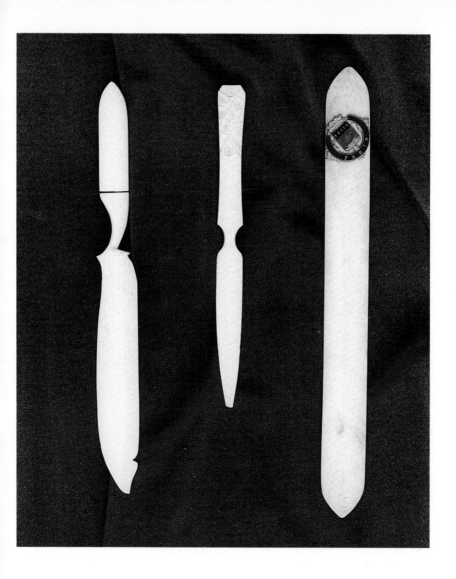

1: Unusual Design; ivory; 8 3/4" $30

2: Indian Style Design; bone; 6 3/4" $15

3: Emblem of Paris; bone; 9 1/2" $20

1: Primitive Vine Design; ivory; 9 1/2" $40

2: Egyptian Figural; ivory; 10 3/4" $60

3: Egyptian Sarcophagus Figural; ivory; 10 1/2" $60

1: Cloaked Woman Figural; hand carved wood; 7 1/4" $15

2: Bearded Gentleman Figural; hand carved wood; 6 1/4" $10

3: Gypsy Figural; hand carved wood; 4 1/2" $10

4: Pirate Figural; hand carved wood; 7"; (paint on blade reads "Ste. Anne de Beaupre'") $15

1: Terrier in Relief; carved wood; 8" $15

2: Tree Branch "Boxer" Carving; natural wood; 7 1/2" $120

3: Small Dog Figural; carved wood; 4 3/4" $20

4: Hawaiian Monkey Figural; carved and finished wood; 8 3/4";
(blade reads "Monkey Pod Wood", "TIKI", "Made in Hawaii") $5

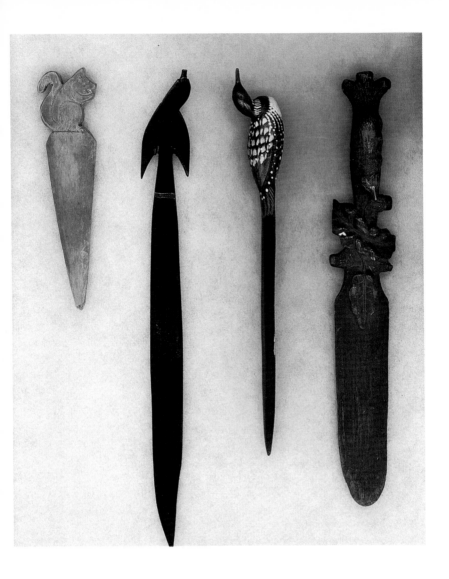

1: Squirrel Figural; hand carved wood; 5" $10

2: Bird Figural; carved teak wood; 10 1/4" $15

3: Duck Figural; painted wood; 8 1/4" $10

4: Opossum & Tree Figural; carved wood; 9" $35

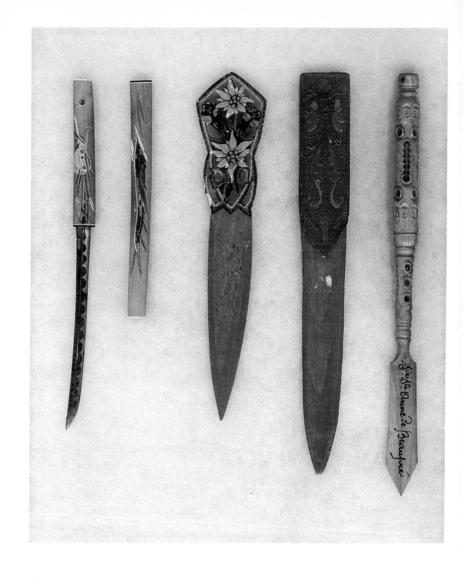

1: Katana (Japanese Sword) Figural w/ scabbard sheath; painted wood & stainless steel blade; 8 1/4"; (Made in Japan) $5

2: Floral Motif; painted wood; 7 3/8" $5

3: Pebbled Grain Floral Design; wood and leather handle; 8 1/2" $10

4: Intricate Figural Design w/ Stanhope viewer; wood; 9"; (blade reads "Sainte Anne De Beaupre'") $40

1: Stick Carving; hand carved wood; 7 1/4" $5

2: Knife Figural; wood & pewter; 8 1/2" $30

3: Marlin Inlay; wood, pewter inlay, stainless steel blade; 8 1/2" $10

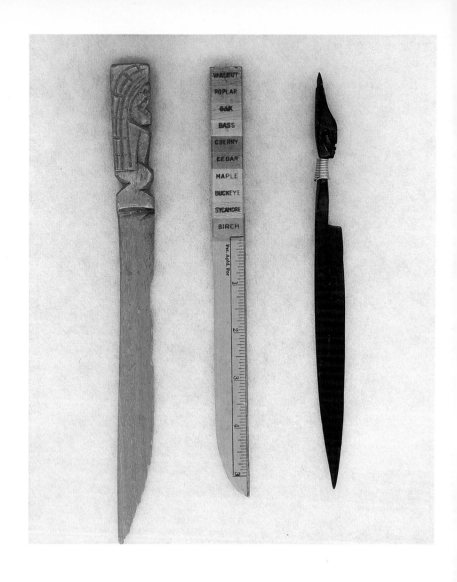

1: Primitive Idol Figural; carved wood; 10 1/4" $10

2: Wooden Display Opener/ Ruler; various woods; 9"; (backside etching reads "Estes Park") $15

3: African Figural Design; teakwood; 9" $10

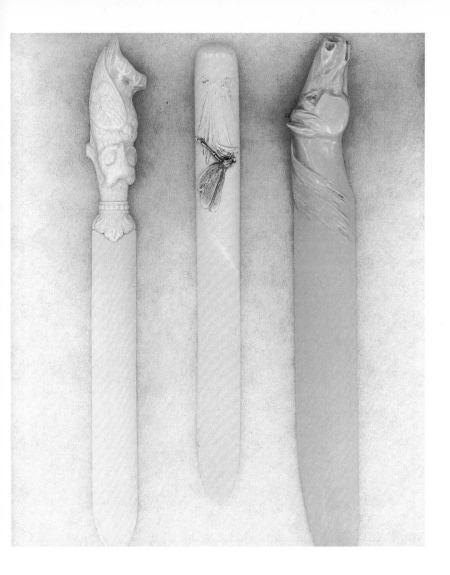

1: Owl Figural; celluloid; 11 1/4" $60

2: Dragonfly Relief Design; celluloid; 9 3/4"; (Made in Germany) $30

3: Horse Head Figural; celluloid; 11 3/4" $50

1: *See Next Page*

2: Elephant Figural; celluloid; 7 1/2"; (Made in Germany) $30

3: Retriever Figural; celluloid; 7 1/2"; (Made in Germany) $30

4: Arctic Owl Figural; celluloid; 8" $30

5: *See Next Page*

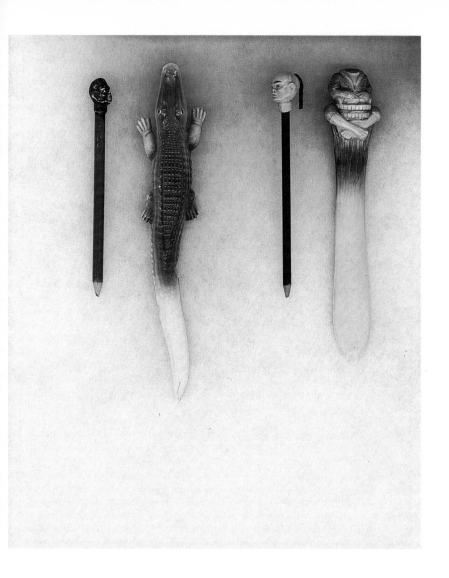

1: Hungry Alligator Figural Opener/ Pencil Holder; celluloid; 7 1/2" $50

2: Chinaman Figural Opener/ Pencil Holder; celluloid; 6 3/4" $50

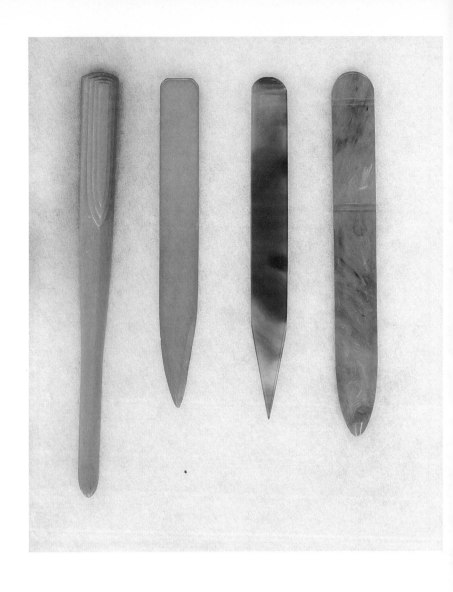

1: Deco Design; Bakelite; 8 3/4" $40

2: Simple Design; Bakelite; 6 3/4" $20

3: Simple Design; Brazilian Agate; 7" $30

4: Simple Design; Bakelite; 7 1/2" $30

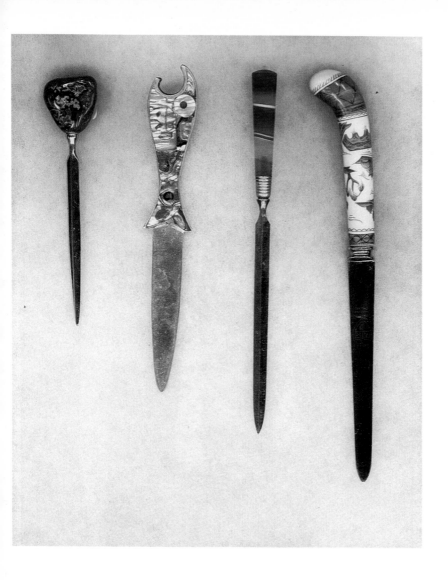

1: Mounted Stone; stainless steel blade; 5 1/4" $15

2: Fish Figural Letter Opener/ Bottle Opener; stainless steel and
mussel shell coated handle; 7" $10

3: Simple Design; stainless steel and agate handle; 7 5/8" $20

4: Nautical Design; stainless steel and porcelain handle; 8 3/4"; (Mfg:
PRILL Sheffield England); (possibly from a gift set) $50

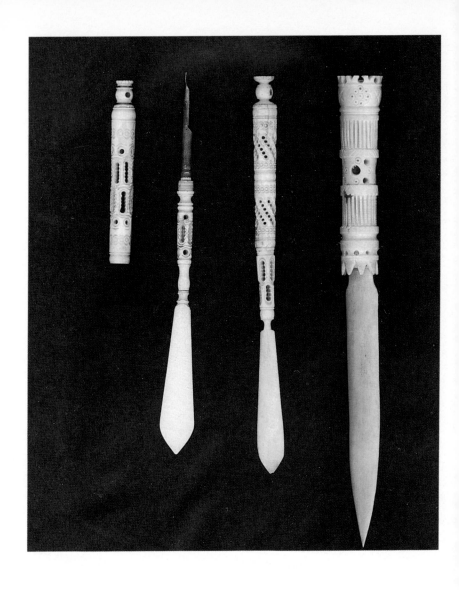

1: Intricate Design Opener/ Quill Pen w/ Stanhope viewer; plastic; 9 1/4" $40

2: Souvenir Opener/ Quill Pen w/ Stanhope viewer; plastic; 8 1/2" $40

3: Intricate Design; plastic; 10" $25

1: Floral Design; plastic w/ leather sheath; 9" $10

2: Deco Motif; plastic; 8 1/2" $5

3: Walnut Inlay; celluloid, walnut, and plastic blade; 8 3/4" $15

4: Intricate Floral Figural; plastic; 10 1/4" $25

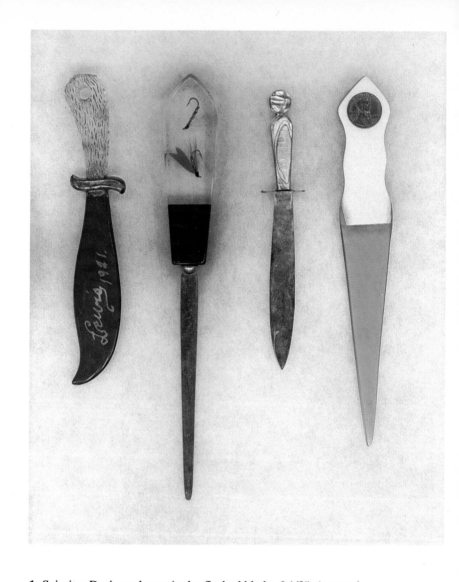

1: Scimitar Design; glass w/ ruby flashed blade; 6 1/2"; (scraped blade reads "Lewis 1921")　　$25

2: Fisherman's Fly; Lucite and stainless steel blade; 9"; (Made in USA)　　$30

3: Sword Design; mussel shell and stainless steel blade; 6"; (Made in Mexico)　　$10

4: Wheat Penny Inset; plastic and 1961 wheat penny; 8"　　$10

1: "Indianapolis Indian" w/ tassel; plastic; 7 1/2"; (blade reads "Indianapolis, Ind.") $20

2: Angry Indian Chief; plastic; 6 1/8" $5

3: Frowning Indian Chief; plastic; 5 1/2" $5

4: Wild Indian; plastic; 6 5/8"; (blade reads "Saugatuck, Mich.") $10

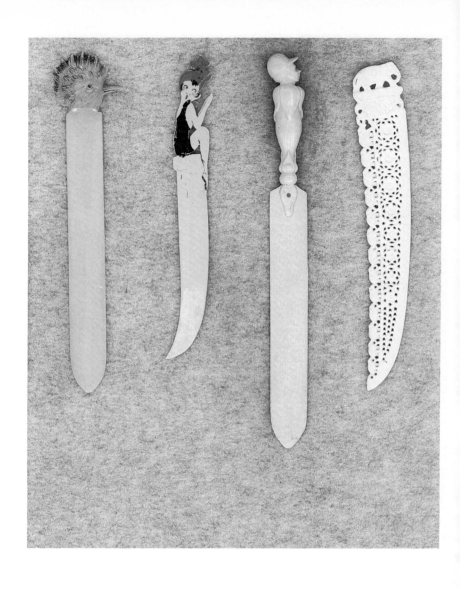

1: Bird Head Figural; celluloid; 7" $10

2: Flapper Figural; painted plastic; 6 1/2" $10

3: Odd Man Figural; plastic w/ celluloid grain texture; 8 1/4" $15

4: Parade of Pachyderms; plastic; 6 1/2"; (Note: extremely mass-produced) $2

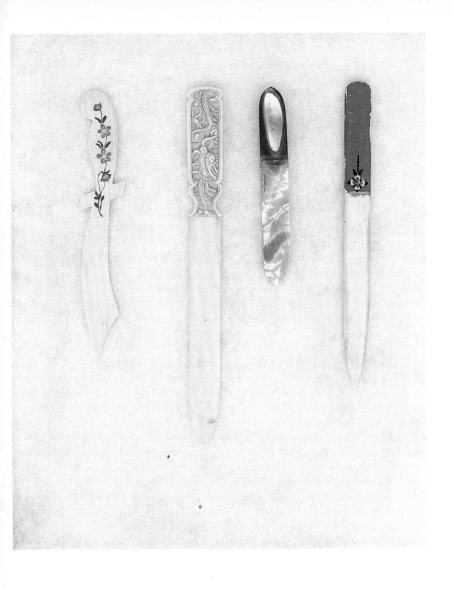

1: Scimitar Figural w/ floral handle; painted celluloid; 5 1/2" $15

2: Chinese Dragon Relief; plastic; 7 1/4"; (Made in China) $20

3: Simple Shape; mussel shell; 4" $10

4: Simple Design; painted plastic; 6 1/2" $5

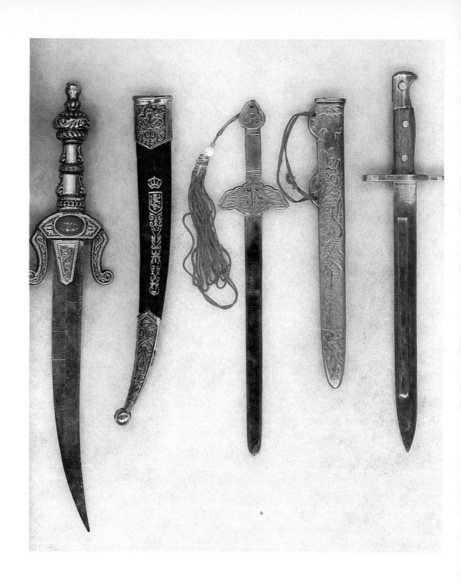

1: Middle Eastern Sword w/ scabbard; steel and leather; 9 1/2" $25

2: Sword Design w/ scabbard and tassels; brass; 8 1/2" $25

3: WWII Bayonet Design; stainless steel and wood; 8"; (Made in Germany) $35

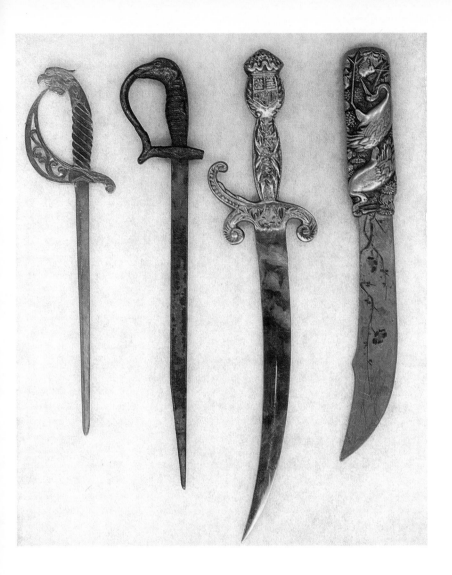

1: Eagle Hilt Sword; tin; 8"; backside reads "Muckle's Pat. Aug 12, 80. Manf'd By Jos. J. Waltonn" $25

2: Sword Design; cast iron; 9" $40

3: Intricate Dagger Design; brass; 10 1/2" $25

4: Intricate Bird Relief; brass; 8 3/4" $25

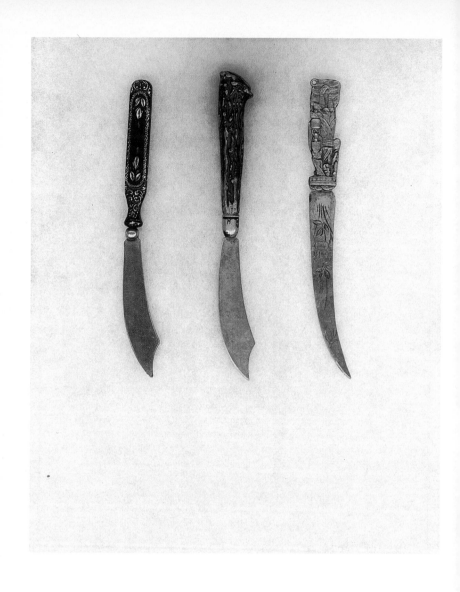

1: Scimitar Style Design; steel and lead handle; 6 1/2" $10

2: Scimitar Style Design; steel and antler handle; 6 3/4" $10

3: Dagger Design w/ nomadic relief; brass; 6 1/4" $20

1: Trench Art Scimitar Design; brass; 7 1/2" $25

2: Trench Art Scimitar Design; brass; 7 1/2"; (blade reads "Sir De France") $25

3: Trench Art Curved Blade; brass; 8"; (blade reads "Cherboug 1944") $25

ADVERTISING LETTER OPENERS

1: "A. Burdsal Co., Indianapolis, IN. 75th Anniversary 1867-1942"; copper; 8"; (Mfg: Metal Arts Co., Rochester, NY) $25

2: "Auto Compressor Co., Wilmington, Ohio"); bronze; 7" $15

3: "Chas. Alshuler Mfg. Co, Racine, Wis."; brass w/ porcelain medallion; 9" $40

4: "Anderson Box Co., Indianapolis, Ind."; brass, 7 3/4" $15

1: "Art Type Company"; copper; 8"; (Mfg: Brown & Bigelow, St. Paul, Minn.) $15

2: "Argenzio Brothers- Fine Jewelers"; brass; 8"; (Made in Japan) $10

3: "L.J. Baker Specialty Co., Des Moines, Iowa"; brass; 4 3/4" $10

4: Cadillac Emblem; bronze; 9 1/4"; (Mfg: G. Fox Co., Cincinnati, Ohio) $100

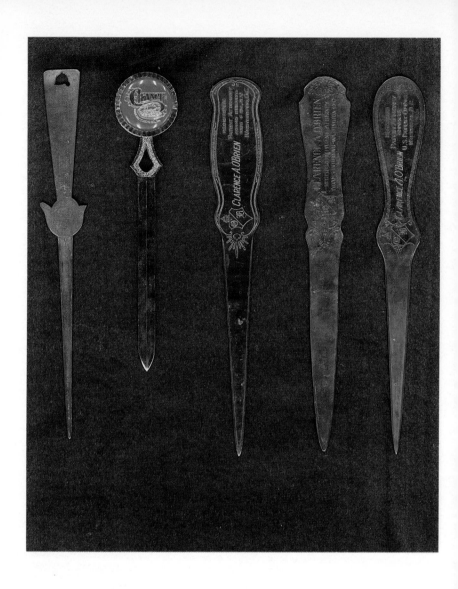

1: "C.H. Besly & Co., Chicago, Ill."; bronze; 7 3/4" $30

2: "Chance Manufacturing Co., Inc."; brass plated; 6 1/4" $10

3-5: "Clarence A. O'Brien, Patent Attorney, Washington DC"
  3: bronze; 8"; (Mfg: J.E. Mergott Co., Newark, NJ) $10
  4: brass; 8"; (Mfg: Metal Arts Co., Rochester, NY) $10
  5: copper; 8" $10

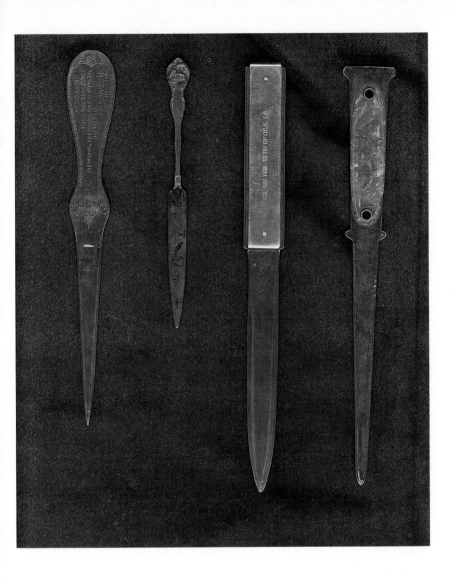

1: "Commercial Auto Service Inc."; bronze; 7 7/8" $10

2: "Culver Military School"; bronze; 5 3/4" $10

3: "Dalton-Webb Optical Co."; steel w/ bronze blade; 9"; (Mfg: Brown & Bigelow, St. Paul, Minn) $15

4: "Daily Democrat, Shelbyville, IN"; plastic w/ copper plated blade; 8 7/8" $10

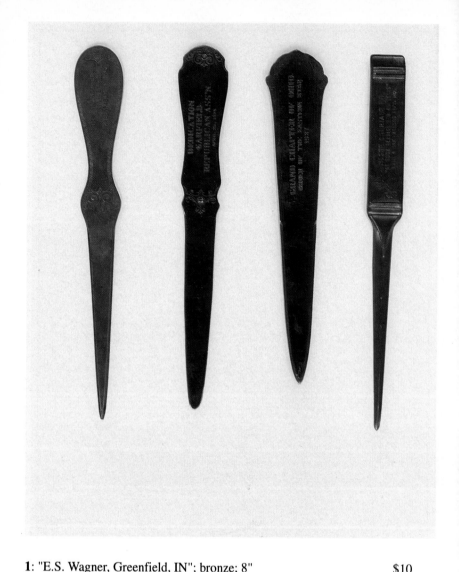

1: "E.S. Wagner, Greenfield, IN"; bronze; 8" $10

2: "Dedication Garfield Republican Assoc., April 25, 1929"; bronze; 7 3/4"; (Mfg: Metal Arts Co., Rochester, NY) $30

3: "Grand Chapter of Ohio- Order of the Eastern Star"; bronze; 7"; (Mfg: American Art Works, Coshocton, OH); (ca.1937) $10

4: "Hesse Carriage Co., Kansas City, MO"; bronze; 8"; (Mfg: Brown & Bigelow Co.; St. Paul, Minn.) $35

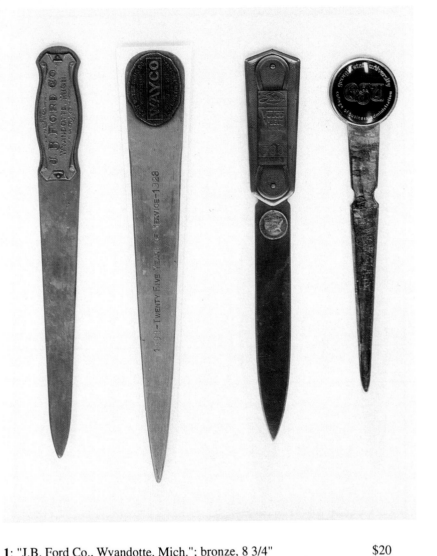

1: "J.B. Ford Co., Wyandotte, Mich."; bronze, 8 3/4" $20

2: "Fort Wayne Drug Co., Ft. Wayne, Ind- 25 Years of Service 1898-1923"; bronze; 8 1/4" $25

3: "Gates Rubber Co.- Vulco V-Belt"; bronze; 8 1/4"; (Mfg: Whitehead & Hoag Co., Newark, NJ) $40

4: "Georgia State University"; bronze; 7" $10

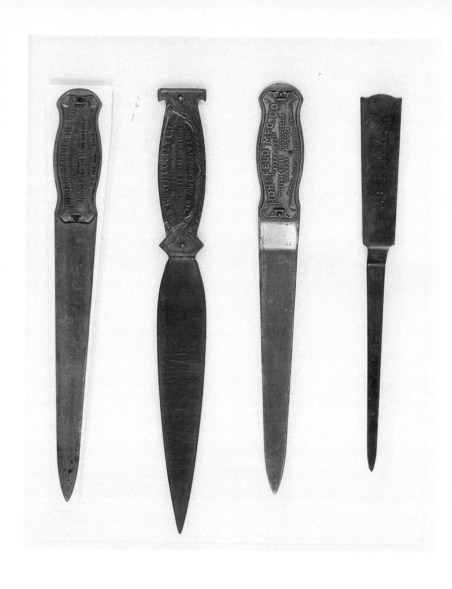

1: "H.H. Baumgartner Mfg. Co., Geneva, IN"; bronze; 8 3/4"; (Mfg: J.E. Mergott Co., Newark, NJ); (ca. 1930) $15

2: "Hart & Cooley Co. Inc., New Britain, CT"; bronze; 9 1/2" $25

3: "Hohlfeld Mfg. Co., Philadelphia, PA"; bronze; 8 3/4" $15

4: Monogrammed "I.I.E.A."; bronze; 8" $5

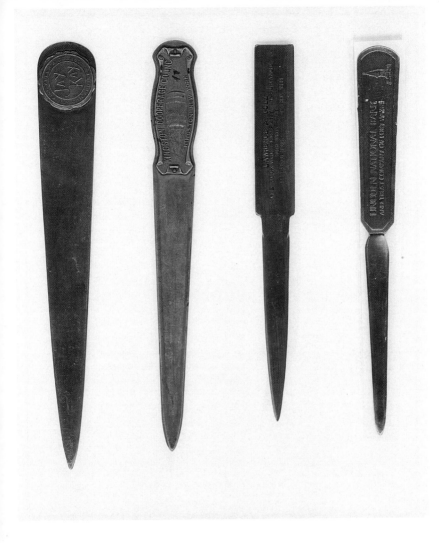

1: "Jay Kay"; bronze; 9"; (Mfg: Metal Arts Co., Rochester, NY) $10

2: "Kingston Cooperage Co., Inc., Kingston, NY"; bronze; 8 1/2";
(Mfg: J.E. Mergott Co.) $30

3: "Lawrence A. Golz, Rockwood Co. Ins."; bronze; 8" $5

4: "Lincoln National Bank & Trust Co., Ft. Wayne, IN"; bronze;
8 1/4" $5

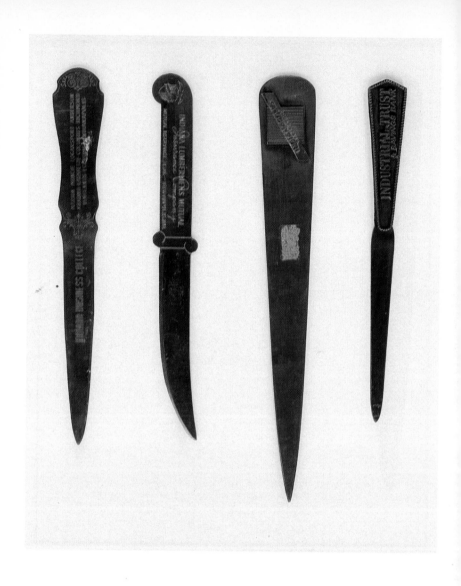

1: "Indiana Business College"; bronze; 8"; (Mfg: Metal Arts Co., Rochester, NY) $10

2: "Indiana Lumbermen's Mutual Insurance Co."; bronze; 7 3/4" $5

3: "Indianapolis Separators"; bronze; 9" $15

4: "Industrial Trust & Savings Bank"; bronze; 7 1/4" $5

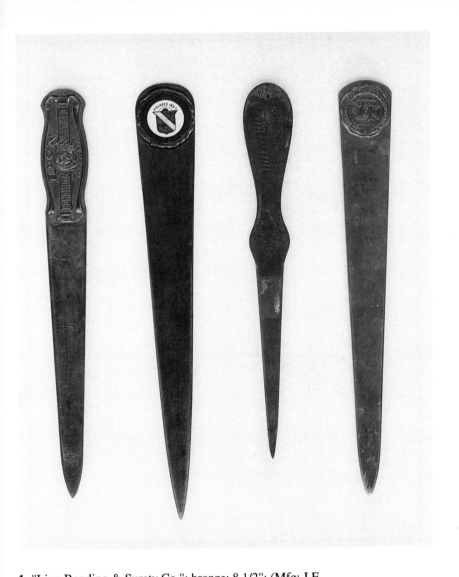

1: "Lion Bonding & Surety Co."; bronze; 8 1/2"; (Mfg: J.E. Mergott Co., Newark, NJ) $15

2: "McCann School"; bronze; 9 1/4"; (Mfg: W.B-H. Co., Newark, NJ) $25

3: "Milwaukee Lace Paper Co."; bronze; 8" $15

4: "Metropolitan Life Insurance Co."; bronze; 8 3/4"; (Mfg: Whitehead & Hoag Co., Newark, NJ) $20

1: "Middle West Coal Co., Cincinnati, Ohio"; copper w/ steel blade; 9" $45

2: "Moor Mud Baths, Waukesha, Wisconsin"; bronze; 8 1/2" $15

3: "NCR Openhouse 1951"; bronze; 5 1/8" $15

4: "NCR"; bronze; 8 1/4"; (ca. 1953) $10

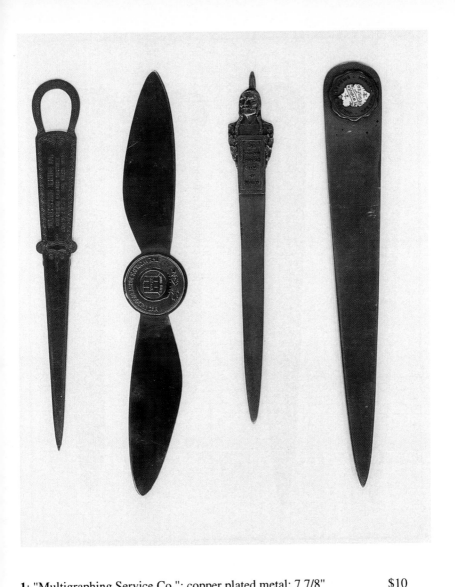

1: "Multigraphing Service Co."; copper plated metal; 7 7/8" $10

2: "Nash 'Airflite' the World's Most Modern Car"; brass; 9" $50

3: "National Shawmut Bank of Boston"; bronze; 7 3/8"; (Mfg: Robbins & Co.) $20

4: "New Haven Register"; bronze; 9"; (Mfg: Metal Arts Co., Rochester, NY) $15

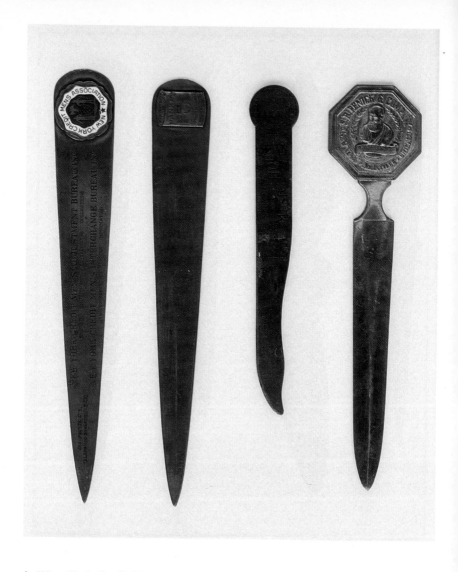

1: "New York Credit Men's Association"; bronze; 9"; (Mfg: House of Advertising Specialties N.Y.C.) $30

2: "L-H Parke Company"; bronze; 9"; (Mfg: Metal Arts Co., Rochester, NY) $40

3: "Pearson Piano Co., Indianapolis, IN"; bronze; 7" $15

4: "S.B. Pennick & Company"; brass; 8 1/2" $10

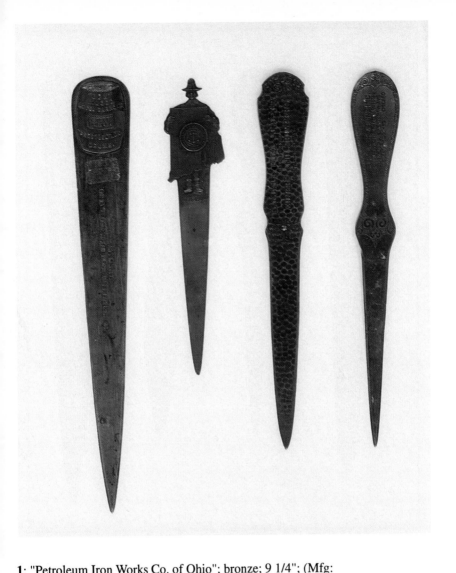

1: "Petroleum Iron Works Co. of Ohio"; bronze; 9 1/4"; (Mfg: Whitehead & Hoag Co., Newark, NJ) $30

2: "Providence Engineering Society 1636-1936"; bronze; 6 1/2" $25

3: "Randall Fuel Company"; bronze; 8"; (Mfg: Metal Arts Co., Rochester, NY) $10

4: "Rossbach & Sons Inc. - Iron Works"; bronze; 8" $10

1: "Rotary International", bronze; 8 3/4" $5

2: "Russet Cafeteria"; bronze; 7 3/4" $15

3: "Tribune Publishing Company- Loogootee, Indiana"; bronze; 8" $15

4: "William Skinner & Sons 100th Anniversary - 1948"; bronze;
9 1/4"; (Mfg: Whitehead & Hoag Co., Newark, NJ) $25

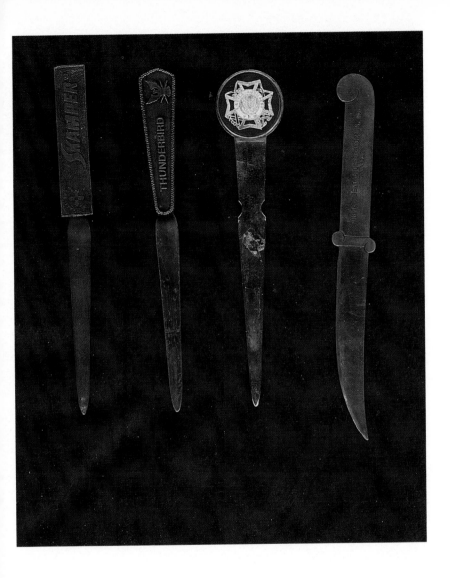

1: "Skamper - AMF"; metal; 7 1/4" $10

2: "Thunderbird - 8th Annual Dealer Meeting"; metal; 7 1/4" $10

3: "V.F.W. Ladies Auxiliary"; stainless steel; 7" $5

4: "United Dental Laboratories Inc. - Indianapolis, Ind."; bronze;
7 3/4" $15

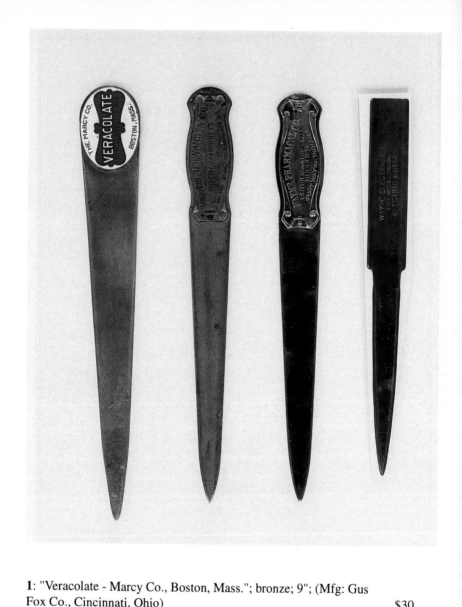

1: "Veracolate - Marcy Co., Boston, Mass."; bronze; 9"; (Mfg: Gus Fox Co., Cincinnati, Ohio) $30

2: "Victor J. Evans Co. - Patent Attorneys"; bronze; 8 3/4 $20

3: "Wayne Pharmacal Co. - Fort Wayne, Indiana"; brass; 8 1/2" $35

4: "Wayne Electrical Co. - Fort Wayne, Indiana"; bronze; 8 1/4" $35

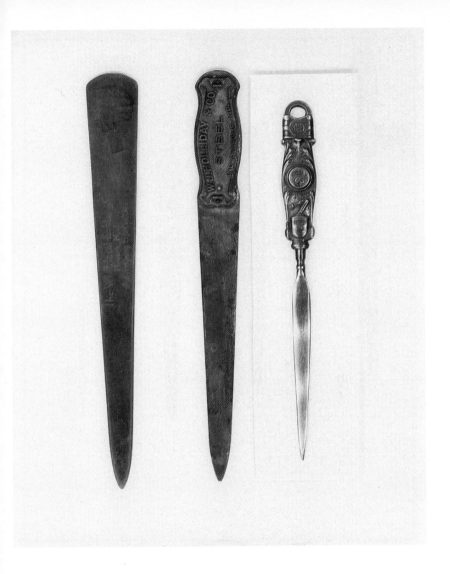

1: "Whitehead & Hoag Co.- Advertising Specialties"; bronze; 8 3/4";
(Mfg: Whitehead & Hoag Co., Newark, NJ) $40

2: "W.S. Holliday & Co. - Steel"; bronze; 8 3/4" $20

3: "Yale & Towne Mfg. Co."; bronze w/ stainless steel blade; 8 1/4" $100

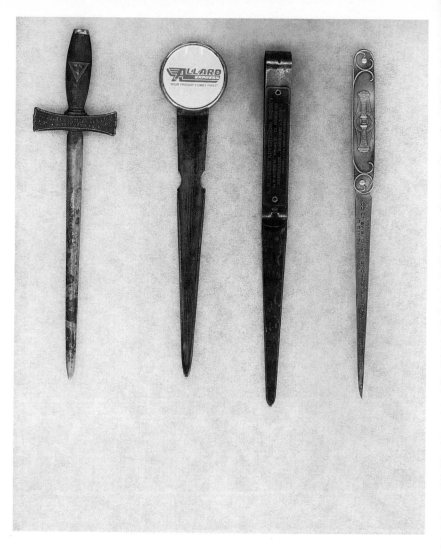

1: "Allegheny Lumber Company - Pittsburgh, PA"; aluminum w/ steel blade; 7 3/8" $30

2: "Allard Express"; stainless steel; 7" $10

3: "A.N. Baker Advertising Agency - Chicago, IL"; tin; 7 1/2" $15

4: "Telephone Improvement Co. - Chicago, IL"; aluminum w/ stainless steel blade; 7 3/8" $20

1: "Bastian Bros. Co.- Rochester, N.Y."; brass w/ plated steel coating; 9" $50

2: "Berry Bros. LTD Varnish Manufacturers - Detroit"; aluminum w/ stainless steel blade; 8 1/4" $20

3: Same as **2** but has inverted copper handle $20

4: "Bibi & Company - House of Fine Crystal"; aluminum; 8"; (Mfg: Louis F. Dow Co.; St. Paul, Minn.) $10

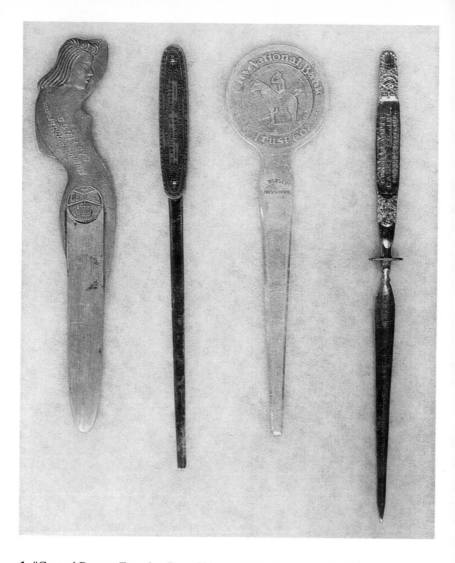

1: "Central Pattern Foundry Co. - Chicago, Ill."; aluminum; 8 1/4" $45

2: "Century of Progress - Chicago 1934"; stainless steel; 9"; (Note: World's Fair souvenir); (Made in Czechoslovakia) $15

3: "City National Bank & Trust Co. - Kansas City, Missouri"; aluminum; 9 1/2" $10

4: "Connersville Casket Co., Inc. - Connersville, Ind."; stainless steel; 10" $15

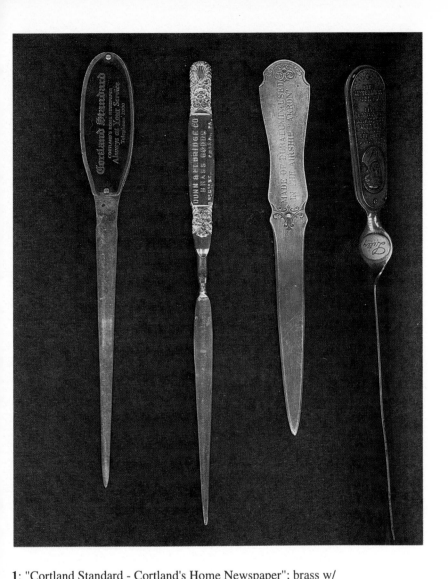

1: "Cortland Standard - Cortland's Home Newspaper"; brass w/ stainless steel blade; 9 1/4" $15

2: "Dunn & Eldridge Co. Brass Goods - Phila., PA"; stainless steel; 9 3/4" $10

3: "Made of Duralumin used in the airship 'Akron'"; Duralumin; 7 7/8" $75

4: "Eli Lilly & Company - Indianapolis, Ind., 50th Anniversary 1876-1926"; brass w/ stainless steel blade; 10" $50

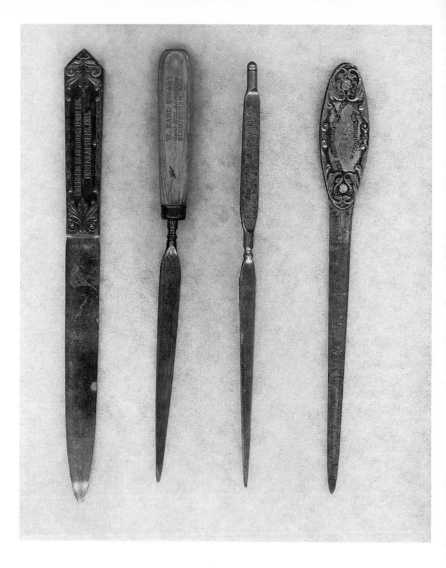

1: "Emerson-Scheuring Tank Co. - Indianapolis, IN"; brass w/ stainless steel blade; 9 1/2" $15

2: "W. Earl Ewart - Good Will Advertising, Birmingham, Ala."; wood w/ steel blade; 9" $40

3: "E.D. Fearing"; stainless steel; 9" $10

4: "First National Bank - Pittsburgh, PA"; pewter w/ steel blade; 9 1/8" $20

1: "Phoenix Tannery - Allegheny, PA"; tin and steel; 8"; (Mfg: Wilbur P. Co. of Chicago); (ca. 1895) $75

2: "Gilliam Mfg. Co. - Canton, Ohio"; tin and steel; 8"; (Mfg: Wilbur P. Co. of Chicago); (ca. 1895) $75

3: "E.F. Hallock Lumber and Mfg. Co. - Denver, Colorado"; tin and steel; 8"; (Mfg: Wilbur P. Co. of Chicago); (ca. 1895) $75

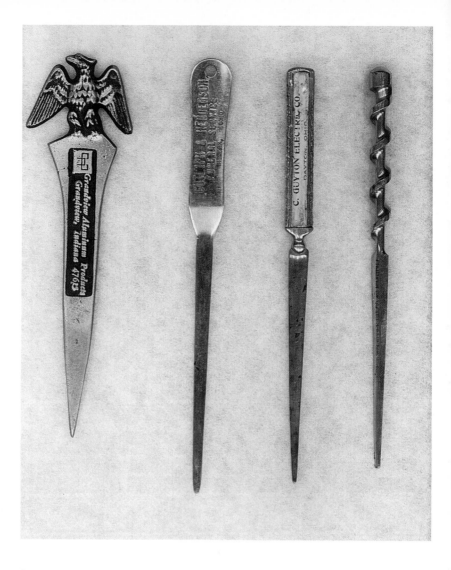

1: "Grandview Aluminum Products - Grandview, Ind."; aluminum; 8" $10

2: "Gutliph & Henderson Funeral Service - Newark, Ohio"; stainless steel; 9 1/4" $15

3: "C. Guyton Electric Co. - Dayton, Ohio"; lithographed tin w/ steel blade; 8 3/4" $40

4: "Irwin Auger Bit Co. - Wilmington, Ohio"; stainless steel; 8 1/2" $15

1: "Joseph R. Peeble's Sons Co. - Cincinnati, Ohio"; metal; 6 3/8";
(ca. 1880) $75

2: "Knights of St. John - Supreme Ladies Auxiliary"; plastic &
stainless steel blade; 7" $10

3: "Life Indemnity Co. - Knights, Templars, and Masons - Chicago,
Ill"; stainless steel; 9 1/2" $20

4: "Lions International"; aluminum; 8 1/2" $15

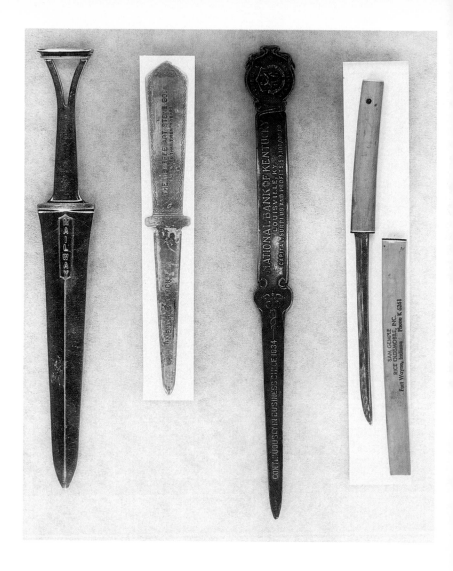

1: "Mailway" Dagger Figural ; chromed metal; 9 1/4" $5

2: "Menefee Artstone Co."; aluminum; 7"; (ca. 1910) $20

3: "National Bank of Kentucky - Louisville, KY"; nickel plated
bronze; 10" $35

4: "Rice Oldsmobile, Inc - Ft. Wayne, Indiana" Katana Figural;
wood w/ metal blade; 8 1/4"; (ca. 1955) $10

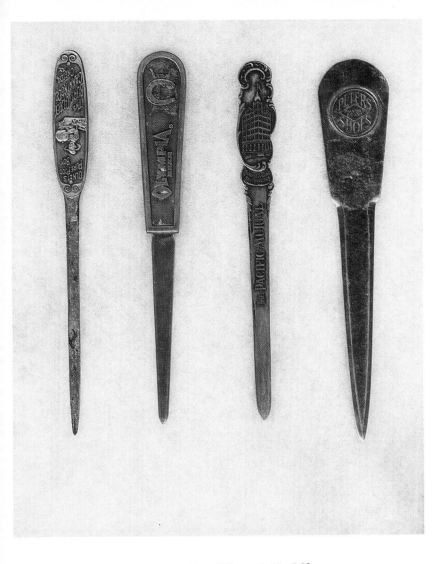

1: "Burt Olney Canning Co. - Oneida, NY"; steel; 8"; (Mfg: Magnetic Cutlery Co., Phila. PA $35

2: "Olympia Beer"; pewter w/ steel blade; 7 1/4" $15

3: "Pacific Mutual"; nickel; 7 1/2" $30

4: "Peter's Shoes"; stainless steel; 8" $45

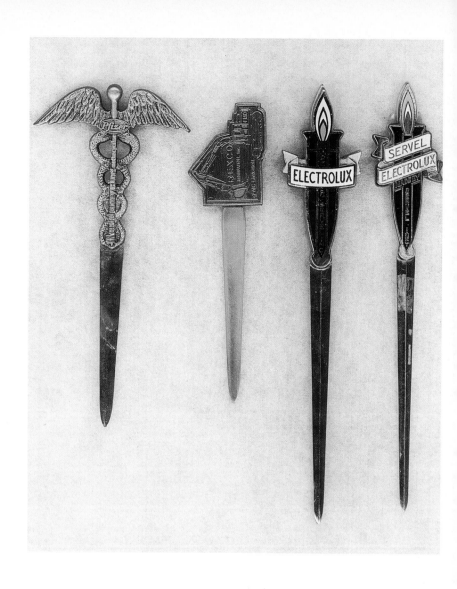

1: "Pfizer Rondomycin"; stainless steel; 7 1/4" $20

2: "Rexco Equipment"; pewter w/ steel blade; 6 3/8" $10

3: "Electrolux/ Servel Inc."; chromed steel, paper, plastic; 9 1/4" $30

4: "Electrolux/ Servel Inc."; chromed steel, paper, plastic; 9" $25

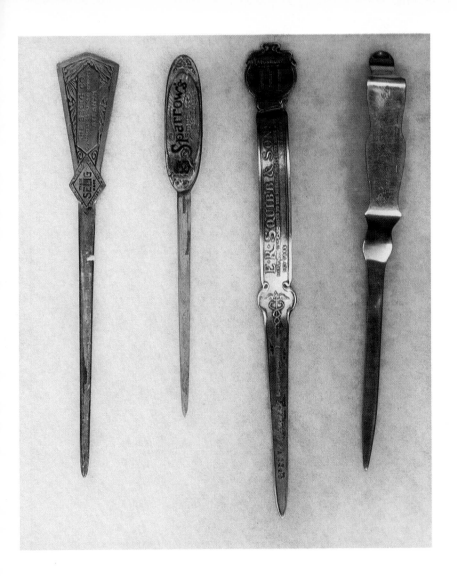

1: "Selig Co.- Atlanta"; steel; 9" $15

2: "Sparrow's Empress Chocolates"; steel; 7 5/8"; (Mfg: Robbins USA) $25

3: "E.R. Squibb & Sons"; steel; 10" $50

4: "Chas. G. Stevens Co."; stainless steel; 8 3/4" $15

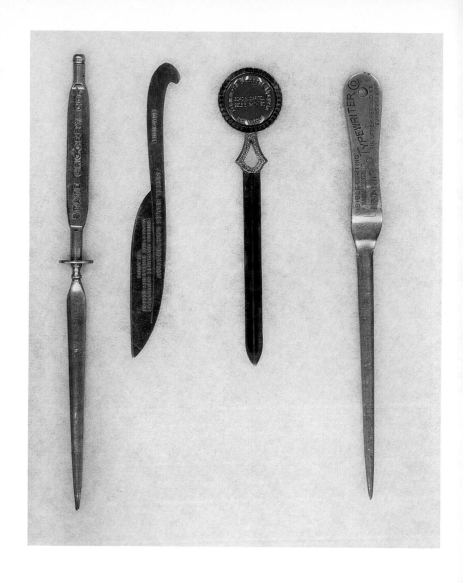

1: "State Grocery Co."; steel; 9 1/2" $10

2: "Steel Sales Corp."; steel; 6 1/4" $10

3: "Summers Funeral Chapels"; steel; 6 1/4" $5

4: "Underwood Typewriter Co."; steel; 9" $20

1: Uneeda Bread Co.; lithographed tin; 8 1/4" $45

2: "USA Track & Field"; stainless steel; 7 3/8"; (Olympic souvenir) $10

3: "E.H. Walker - Contractor - Canton, Ohio"; steel; 9 1/8" $20

4: "Warp Publishing Co. - Minden, Nebr."; stainless steel; 8 1/2" $20

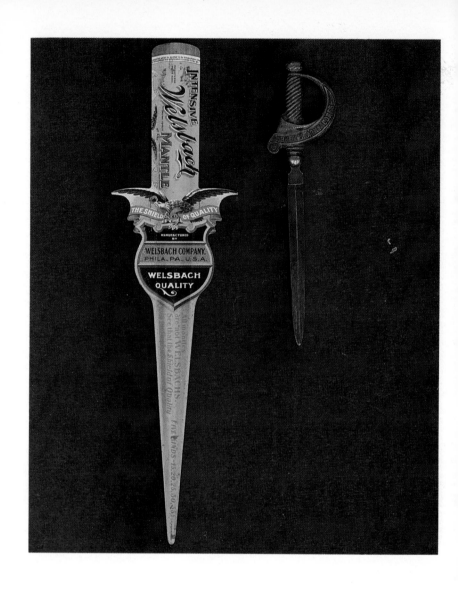

1: "Welsbach Company, Phila., PA"; tin; 10 1/2" $50

2: "Women's Army Corps"; steel; 6" $20

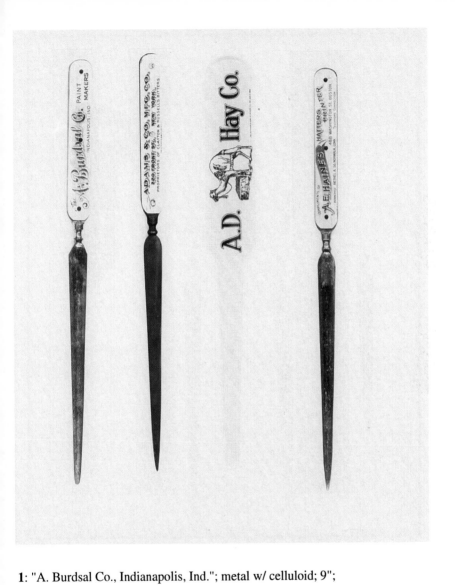

1: "A. Burdsal Co., Indianapolis, Ind."; metal w/ celluloid; 9";
(Mfg: Whitehead & Hoag Co., Newark, NJ); (ca. 1900-1910) $35

2: "Adams & Co. Mfg. Co., New York"; metal w/ celluloid; 9";
(Mfg: Whitehead & Hoag Co., Newark, NJ); (ca. 1900-1910) $45

3: "A.D. Hay Co., Peoria, Ill"; metal w/ celluloid; 8 5/8"; (Mfg:
Whitehead & Hoag Co., NJ); (ca. 1905) $40

4: "A.E. Haines, Boston, Mass."; metal w/ celluloid; 8 7/8" $35

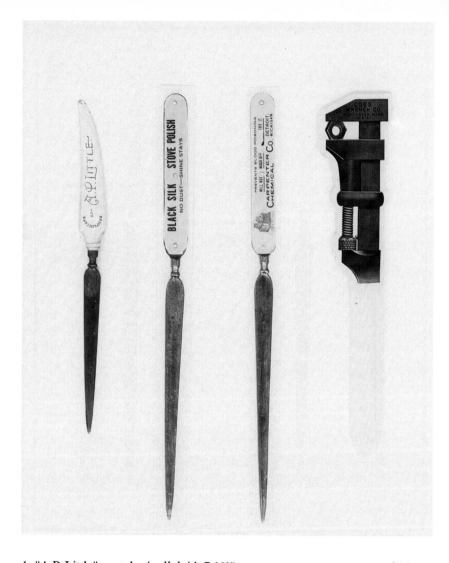

1: "A.P. Little"; metal w/ celluloid; 7 1/4" $35

2: "Black Silk Stove Polish"; metal w/ celluloid; 9"; (Mfg: Meek
Co., Coshocton, Ohio); (ca. 1900-1910) $40

3: "Carpenter Chemical Co., Detroit, Michigan"; metal w/ celluloid;
9"; (ca. 1900-1910) $45

4: " Coes Wrench Co., Worcester, Mass"; celluloid; 7 3/4"; (Mfg:
Whitehead & Hoag Co., Newark, NJ); (ca. 1900-1910) $65

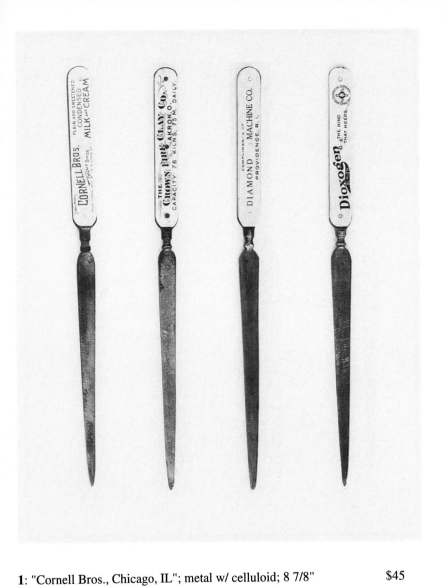

1: "Cornell Bros., Chicago, IL"; metal w/ celluloid; 8 7/8"　　$45

2: "Crown Fire Clay Co.; Akron, Ohio"; metal w/ celluloid; 9";
(Mfg: Whitehead & Hoag Co., Newark, NJ); (ca. 1900-1910)　　$35

3: "Diamond Machine Co., Providence, RI"; metal w/ celluloid;
9"; (Mfg: Meek Co., Coshocton, Ohio); (ca. 1900-1910)　　$35

4: "Dioxogen Oakland Chemical Co."; metal w/ celluloid; 8 7/8";
(Whitehead & Hoag Co., Newark, NJ); (ca. 1900-1910)　　$35

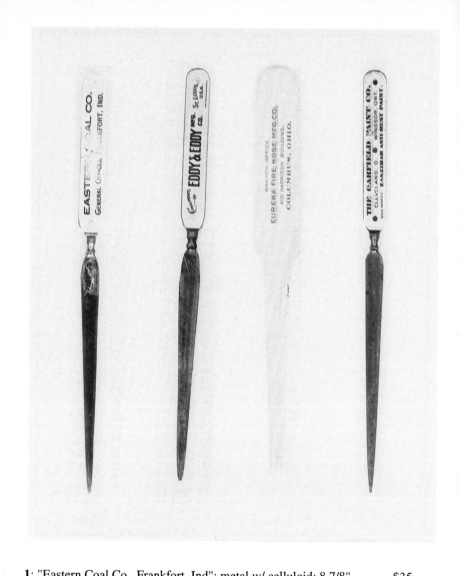

1: "Eastern Coal Co., Frankfort, Ind"; metal w/ celluloid; 8 7/8" $35

2: "Crown Fire Clay Co., Akron, Ohio"; metal w/ celluloid; 9";
(Mfg: Whitehead & Hoag Co., Newark, NJ); (ca. 1900-1910) $35

3: "Diamond Machine Co., Providence, RI"; metal w/ celluloid;
9"; (Mfg: Meek Co., Coshocton, Ohio); (ca. 1900-1910) $35

4: "Dioxogen, Oakland Chemical Co."; metal w/ celluloid; 8 7/8";
(Mfg: Whitehead & Hoag Co., Newark, NJ); (ca. 1900-1910) $35

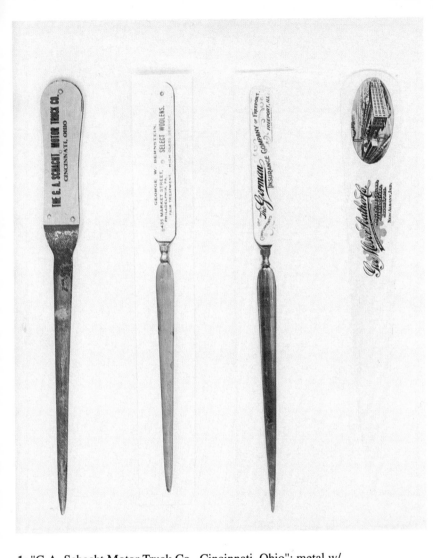

1: "G.A. Schacht Motor Truck Co., Cincinnati, Ohio"; metal w/ celluloid; 9 1/4"; (Mfg: American Art Works, Coshocton, Ohio) $50

2: "Geo. W. Bernstein Select Woolens, Phila., PA"; metal w/ celluloid; 8 3/4"; (Mfg: Whitehead & Hoag Co., Newark, NJ) $35

3: "German Insurance Company of Freeport, Freeport, Ill"; metal w/ celluloid; 9"; (Mfg: Whitehead & Hoag Co., Newark, NJ) $35

4: "Geo. Moser Leather Co., New Albany, Ind."; celluloid; 9 1/4"; (Mfg: Whitehead & Hoag Co., Newark, NJ); (ca. 1910) $60

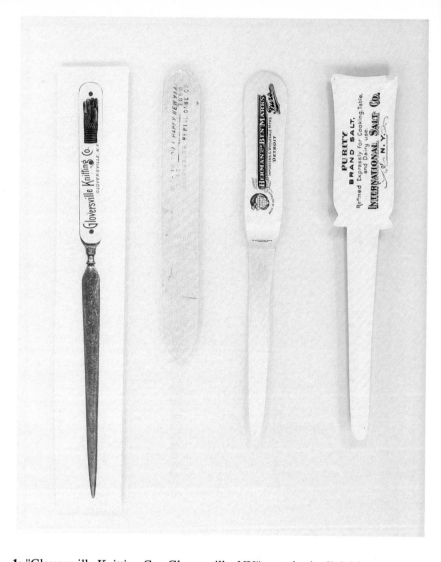

1: "Gloversville Knitting Co., Gloversville, NY"; metal w/ celluloid; 8 3/4"; (Mfg: Whitehead & Hoag Co., Newark; NJ); (ca. 1900-1910) $45

2: "Harrisburg Burial Case Co."; celluloid; 6 1/4"; (ca. 1890) $35

3: "Herman and Ben Marks Furs, Detroit"; celluloid; 8"; (American Art Works, Coshocton, Ohio) $45

4: "International Salt Co., NY"; celluloid; 7 1/2"; (Mfg: Whitehead & Hoag Co., Newark, NJ); (ca. 1920's) $40

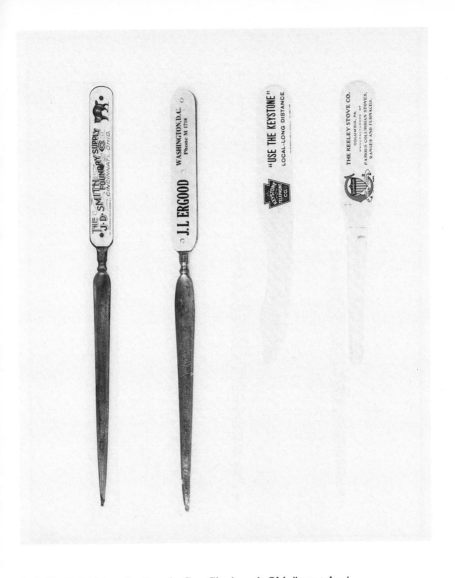

1: "J.D. Smith Foundry Supply Co., Cincinnati, Ohio"; metal w/ celluloid; 8 7/8"; (Mfg: Whitehead & Hoag Co., Newark, NJ)　　　$45

2: "J.L. Ergood, Washington DC"; metal w/ celluloid; 8 7/8"　　　$45

3: "Keystone Telephone Co."; celluloid; 6"; (Whitehead & Hoag Co., Newark, NJ); (ca. 1906)　　　$40

4: "Keeley Stove Co., Columbia, PA"; celluloid; 6"; (Mfg: Whitehead & Hoag Co., NJ)　　　$35

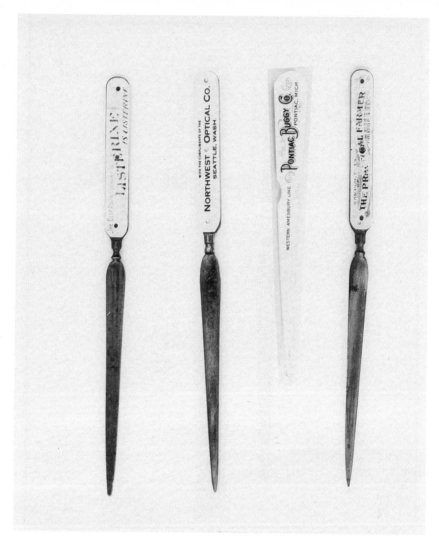

1: "Listerine"; metal w/ celluloid; 8 7/8"; (ca. 1910's) $60

2: "Northwest Optical Co., Seattle, Wash."; metal w/ celluloid;
9"; (Mfg: American Art Works, Coshocton, Ohio); (ca. 1900-1910) $35

3: "Pontiac Buggy Co., Pontiac, Mich."; celluloid; 6 1/2"; (Mfg:
P.F. Pulver Co., Rochester, NY); (ca. 1905) $75

4: "Practical Farmer, Philadelphia, USA"; metal w/ celluloid; (Mfg:
Whitehead & Hoag Co., Newark, NJ); (ca. 1900-1910) $40

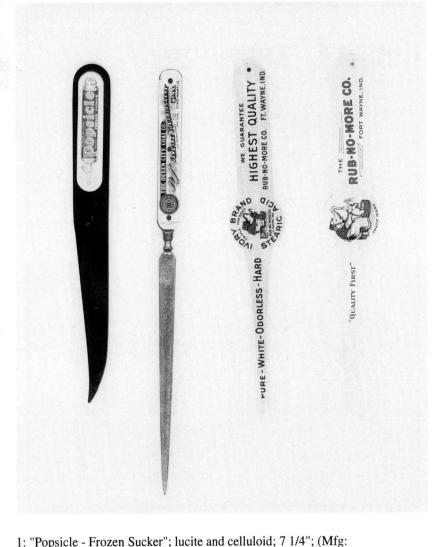

1: "Popsicle - Frozen Sucker"; lucite and celluloid; 7 1/4"; (Mfg: Parisian Novelty Co., Chicago) $30

2: "Queen City Coal Co., Cincinnati, Ohio"; metal w/ celluloid; 9"; (Mfg: Whitehead & Hoag Co., Newark, NJ); (ca. 1900-1910) $45

3: "Rub-No-More Co., Ft. Wayne, Ind."; celluloid; 7 1/2"; (Mfg: Whitehead & Hoag Co., Newark, NJ); (ca. 1910) $125

4: "Rub-No-More Co., Ft. Wayne, Ind."; celluloid; 7 5/8"; (Mfg: Whitehead & Hoag Co., Newark, NJ); (ca. 1910) $125

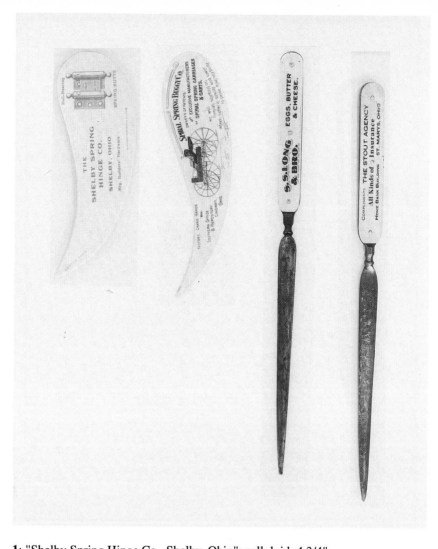

1: "Shelby Spring Hinge Co., Shelby, Ohio"; celluloid; 4 3/4";
(Mfg: Whitehead & Hoag Co., Newark, NJ); (ca. 1905) $60

2: "Spiral Spring Buggy Co."; celluloid; 5"; (Mfg: John A. Lowell
& Co., Boston); (ca. 1900) $125

3: "S.S. Long & Bro."; metal w/ celluloid; 8 7/8"; (Mfg: Whitehead
& Hoag Co., Newark, NJ); (ca. 1900-1910) $45

4: "Stout Agency, St. Marys, Ohio"; metal w/ celluloid; 8 7/8"; (Mfg:
American Art Works Inc., Coshocton, OH); (ca. 1900-1910) $35

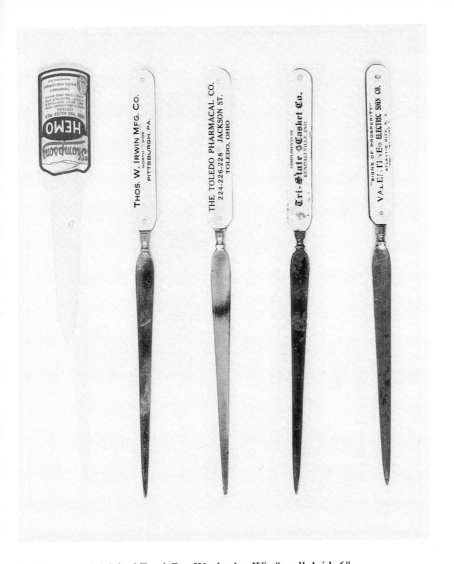

1: "Thompson's Malted Food Co., Waukesha, Wis."; celluloid; 6";
(ca. 1900-1910) $50

2: "Thos. W. Irwin Mfg. Co., Pitts. PA"; metal w/ celluloid; 9";
(Mfg: American Art Works, Coshocton, Ohio); (ca. 1900-1910) $40

3: "Toledo Pharmacal Co., Toledo, Ohio"; metal w/ celluloid; 9";
(Mfg: Whitehead & Hoag Co., Newark, NJ); (ca. 1905) $40

4: "Tri-State Casket Co., Kendallville, Ind."; metal w/ celluloid; 9";
(Mfg: American Art Works Inc., Coshocton, OH); (ca. 1900-1910) $35

5: "Valentine Electric Sign Co., Atlantic City"; metal w/ celluloid;
8 7/8"; (Mfg: Whitehead & Hoag Co., Newark, NJ); (ca. 1906) $40

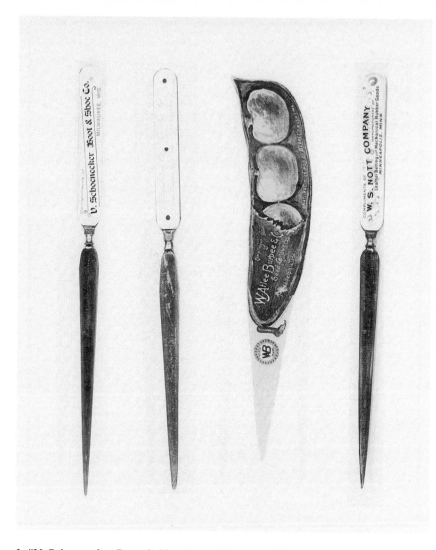

1: "V. Schoenecker Boot & Shoe Co., Milwaukee, Wis."; metal w/ celluloid; 9"; (Mfg: Whitehead & Hoag Co., Newark, NJ); (ca. 1910) $35

2: "Williamsburg City Fire Ins. Co."; metal w/ celluloid; 8 7/8"; (Mfg: J.B. Carroll Co., Chicago); (ca. 1900-1910) $30

3: "W. Atlee Burpee & Co., Philadelphia, PA"; celluloid; 8"; (Mfg: Baldwin & Gleason Co., NY); (ca. 1905) $80

4: "W.S. Nott Co., Minneapolis, Minn."; metal w/ celluloid; 8 7/8"; (Whitehead & Hoag Co., Newark, NJ); (ca. 1900-1910) $35

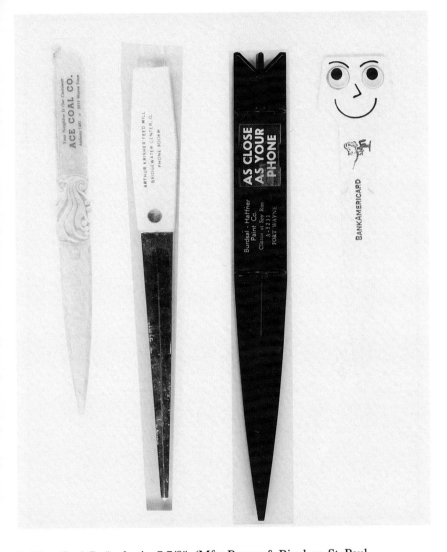

1: "Ace Coal Co."; plastic; 7 7/8"; (Mfg: Brown & Bigelow, St. Paul, MN); (ca. 1940) $15

2: "Arthur Krisher Feed Mill, Bridgewater Center, Ohio"; plastic and metal; 9 1/2"; "Mfg: Autopoint of Chicago"; (ca. 1950) $10

3: "Burdsal-Haffner Paint Co., Ft. Wayne"; plastic; 10"; (1955) $15

4: "Bank Americard"; plastic; 7 1/4"; (1965) $5

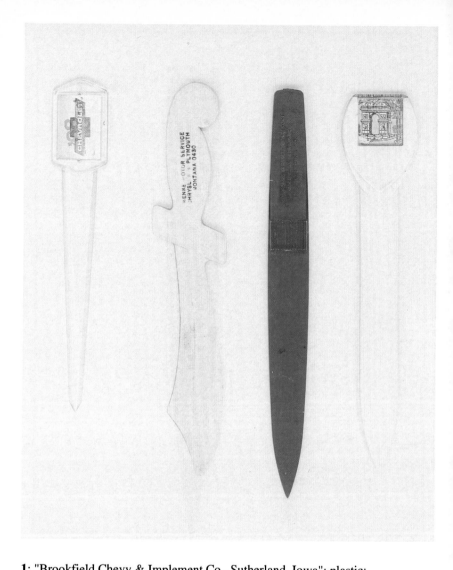

1: "Brookfield Chevy & Implement Co., Sutherland, Iowa"; plastic;
7"; (ca. 1968) $15

2: "Menke Motor Service Chrysler & Plymouth, Montana"; plastic;
8 1/2" $5

3: "C.W. Oldfather, Standard Service to the Home, Westpoint, Ind.";
plastic; 8 3/4" $5

4: "Chunn Perfumes, Paris"; plastic; 8" $10

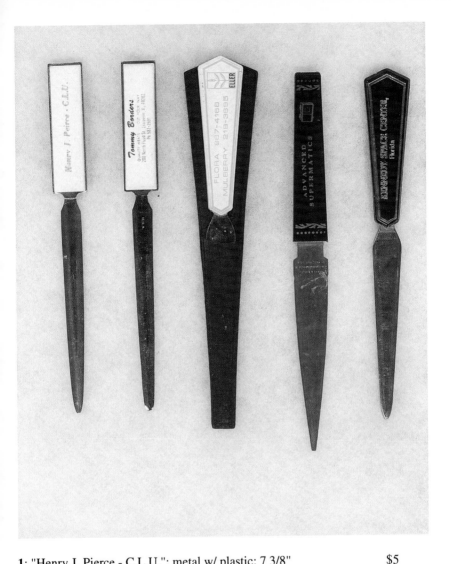

1: "Henry J. Pierce - C.L.U."; metal w/ plastic; 7 3/8" $5

2: "Tommy Borders Quality Meats"; metal w/ plastic; 7 3/8" $5

3: "Eller Seed Co."; metal w/ plastic; 7 1/2" $5

4: "Advanced Supermatics, Maytag Southeastern Co."; metal w/ plastic; 8"; (Mfg: Brown & Bigelow, St. Paul, Minn.) $10

5: "Kennedy Space Center, Florida"; metal w/ plastic; 7 3/8" $15

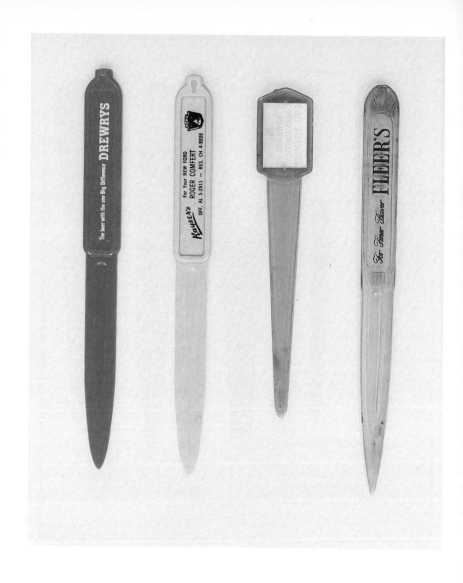

1: "Drewry's Beer"; plastic; 8 1/2" $5

2: "Kayser's Ford"; plastic; 8 1/2" $5

3: "Greenwich Savings Bank, New York"; plastic; 7" $5

4: "Fleers"; plastic; 8 3/4" $30

1: "Fuller Brush Co."; plastic; 7 1/4"; (Note: several color variations may be found) $1

2: "Fuller Brush Co."; plastic; 7 7/8"; (Note: several color variations may be found) $3

3: "Garamycin" Sphinx Figural; plastic; 9" $50

4: "H.K. Kellogg" Chicken Figural; celluloid; 8 5/8" $120

1: "Kennedy Will Win" Campaign Slogan; plastic; 8"; (Note: possibly a reproduction)   original:$25

2: "Langdon Broadcast Advertising Co., Inc."; pewter w/ plastic blade; 8 1/2" $15

3: "Lifetime Electronics, Toledo, Ohio"; plastic; 8 1/2" $10

4: "Miller High Life"; painted plastic; 9" $10

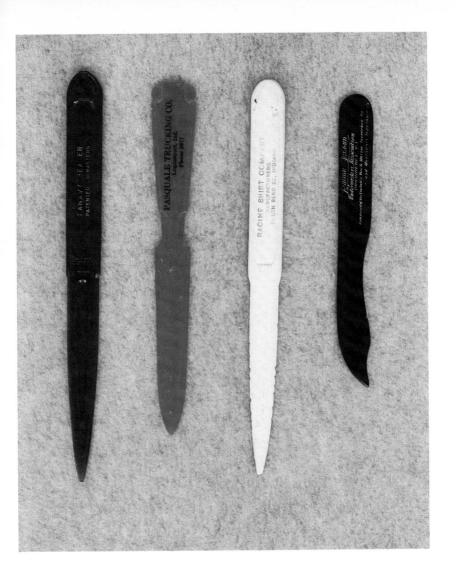

1: "Panama Beaver"; plastic; 8 5/8" $10

2: "Pasquale Trucking Co., Logansport, Ind."; plastic; 7 1/2" $5

3: "Racine Shirt Co., South Bend, Indiana"; plastic; 8 1/4" $10

4: "Rhode Island Underwriters Association"; plastic; 8 1/4" $10

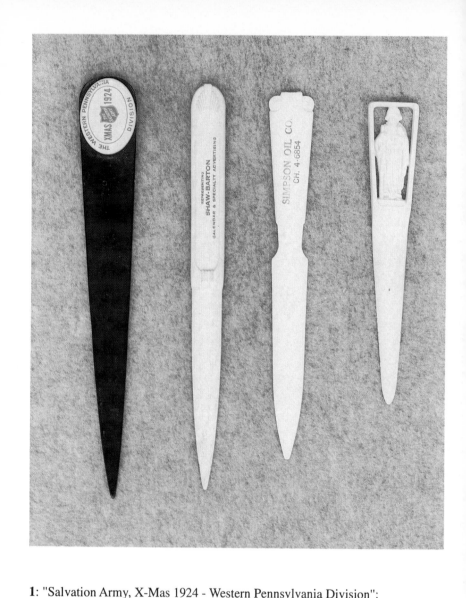

1: "Salvation Army, X-Mas 1924 - Western Pennsylvania Division";
tin & plastic; 8 7/8"; (Mfg: Whitehead & Hoag Co., Newark, NJ) $20

2: "Shaw-Barton Calendar & Specialty Advertising"; plastic; 8 1/2" $5

3: "Simpson Oil Co."; plastic; 7 7/8" $5

4: "St. Jude's Shrine, Baltimore, MD"; plastic; 6 3/8" $5

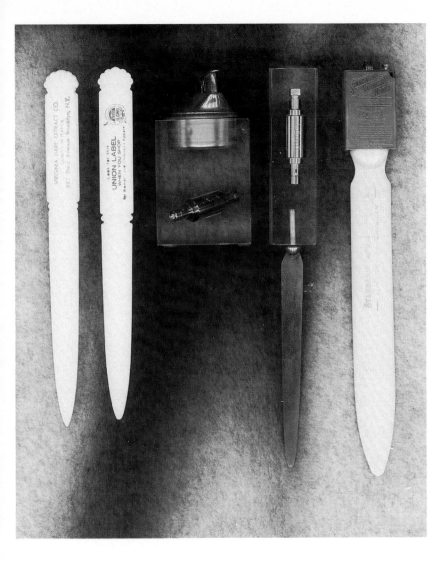

1: "Virginia Dare Extract Co., Brooklyn, NY"; plastic; 7 1/2" $5

2: "Union Label - Garment Workers Union"; plastic; 7 1/2" $5

3-4: "Union" Letter Opener/ Lighter Set; metal w/ lucite; opener is
8 1/2"; lighter is 3 3/4"   set $30

5: "Standard Varnish Works"; celluloid; 8 3/4"; (Mfg: P. Pause &
Co., Chicago) $45

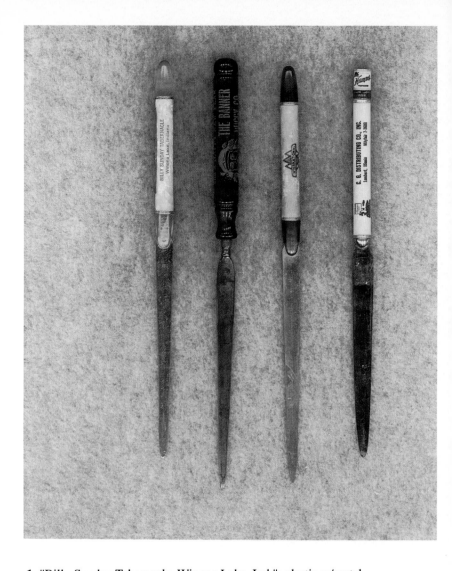

1: "Billy Sunday Tabernacle, Winona Lake, Ind."; plastic w/metal blade; 8 1/4" $10

2: "Banner Buggy Co., St. Louis, MO"; wood w/ metal blade; 9" $50

3: "International -Burley Motor Sales, Highland, Mich."; plastic w/ metal blade; 8 7/8" $15

4: "C.G. Distributing Co., Inc., Lombard, IL- Hamm's Beer"; 8 1/4" $20

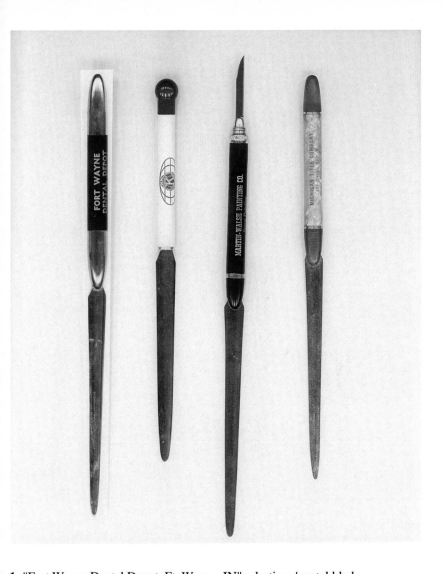

1: "Fort Wayne Dental Depot, Ft. Wayne, IN"; plastic w/ metal blade; 9 1/4"; (ca. 1950) $10

2: "Kiwanis International"; plastic w/ metal blade; 8" $5

3: "Martin-Walsh Painting Co."; plastic and metal; 8 3/4"; (Note: has removable knife on opposite end) $10

4: "Michigan Title Company"; plastic w/ metal blade; 8 3/4" $10

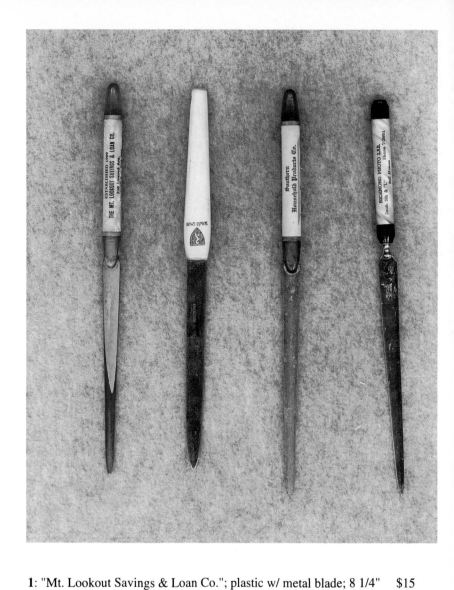

1: "Mt. Lookout Savings & Loan Co."; plastic w/ metal blade; 8 1/4" $15

2: "Ferrari" Emblem; plastic w/ metal blade; 8" $10

3: "Southern Household Products Co., Birmingham, Ala."; plastic
w/ metal blade; 8 1/2" $10

4: "Richmond Photo Lab"; plastic w/ metal blade; 8 1/2" $15

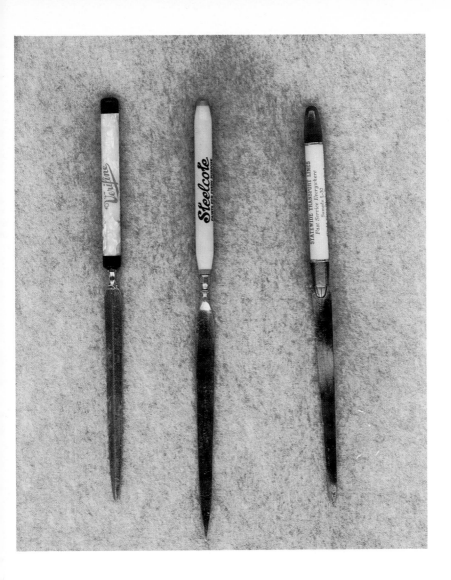

1: "Verifine"; plastic w/ metal; 8 1/2" $10

2: "Steelcote Paints"; plastic w/ metal; 9 1/2" $10

3: "Statewide Transport Lines"; plastic w/ metal; 8 3/8" $10

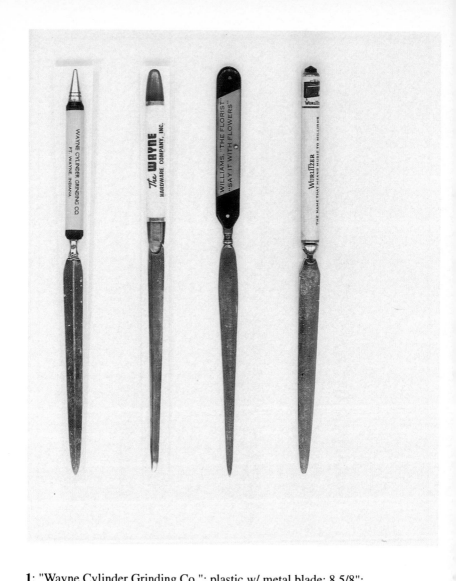

1: "Wayne Cylinder Grinding Co."; plastic w/ metal blade; 8 5/8";
(Note: has retractable pencil on opposite end); (ca. 1955) $15

2: "Wayne Hardware Company Inc."; plastic w/ metal blade; 8 1/2";
(ca. 1950) $10

3: "Williams 'The Florist'"; plastic w/ metal blade; 8 5/8"; (ca. 1955) $10

4: "Wurlitzer- Cumberland Valley Music Co."; plastic w/ metal;
8 1/2"; (Note: has oil pencil on opposite end) $35

1: "Fort McHenry- Baltimore, MD"; copper; 6 1/4"　　　　　　$15

2: "Butte, Montana"; copper; 9 3/8"; (Mfg: Hight & Fairfield)　　$25

3: "San Francisco, California 1915"; copper; 8"　　　　　　$20

4: "Calumet, Mich.- Alex Agassiz 'Founder of the Copper Country'";
copper; 7 3/8"　　　　　　　　　　　　　　　　　　　$25

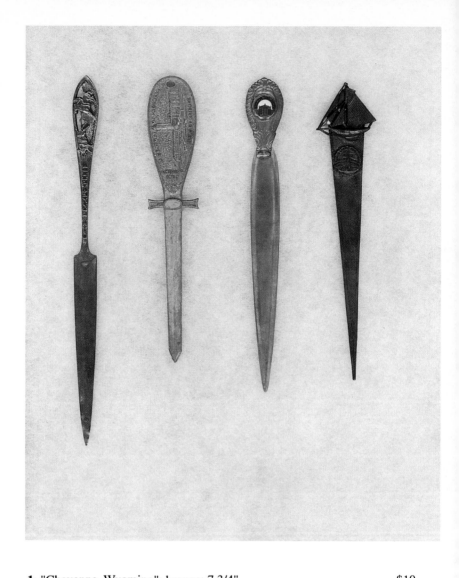

1: "Cheyenne, Wyoming"; bronze; 7 3/4" $10

2: "Century of Progress, Chicago 1933- Hall of Science & Travel &
Transport Bldg."; aluminum; 6"; (Note: World's Fair Souvenir) $25

3: "Chicago Natural History Museum"; bronze w/ nickel finish;
6 1/2" $25

4: "Great Lakes Exposition 1937, Cleveland, Ohio"; bronze; 6 1/4" $20

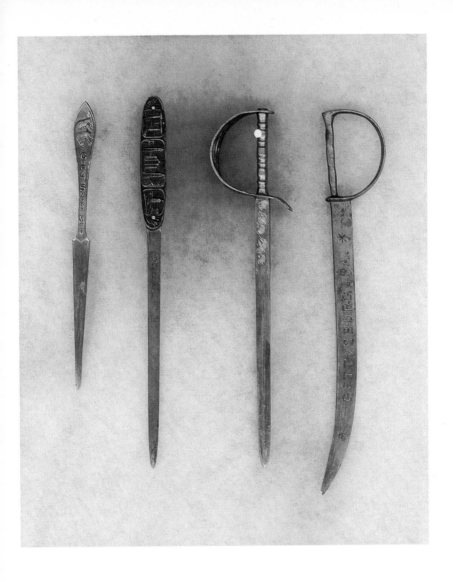

1: "Great Smoky Mts."; bronze; 6 1/8" $10

2: "Souvenir of Habana"; pewter and steel; 7 3/4"; (Mfg: Magnetic
Cutlery Co., Phila., PA) $10

3: "India 44" Sword Figural; brass: 7 1/2" $10

4: "Gettysburg, PA" Sword Figural; brass; 8" $15

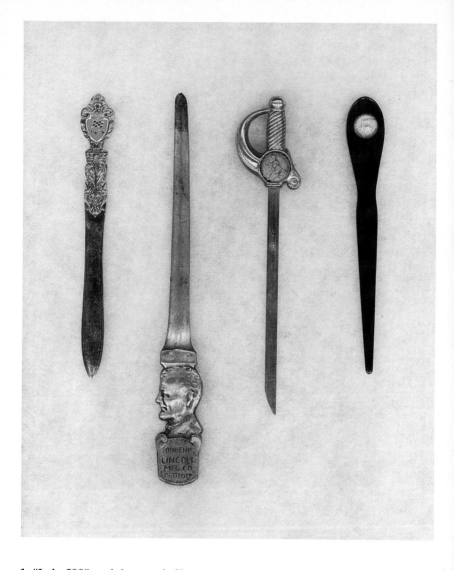

1: "Indy 500"; stainless steel; 6" $10

2: "Souvenir- Lincoln Mfg. Co., Detroit"; plated copper; 8 1/4" $10

3: "Mount Rushmore Coin" Sword Figural; brass w/ stainless steel blade; 6 3/4" $15

4: "World's Fair- New York, Theme Building"; plastic; 5 7/8"; (ca. 1940) $20

1: "World's Fair of 1940 in New York"; stainless steel; 7" $40

2: "North Carolina"; pewter; 6 1/4" $10

3: "Old Sleepy Eye Collectors Convention 1981"; plastic & stainless steel; 7 1/8" $15

4: "Pan-American Souvenir 1901"; forged nail; 5" $25

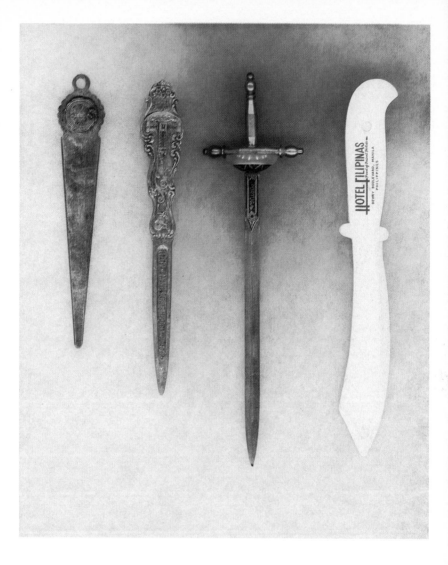

1: "Panama Pacific International Exposition"; bronze w/ stainless
steel finish; 5 3/4"; (Mfg: Bastian Bros. Co., Rochester, NY) $50

2: "Pan-American Exposition 1901"; bronze w/ nickel finish; 6 3/4" $40

3: "Portugal" Sword Figural; brass, plastic, and stainless steel; 8 1/4" $10

4: "Souvenir of Hotel Filipinas- Manila, Phillipines"; plastic; 8" $5

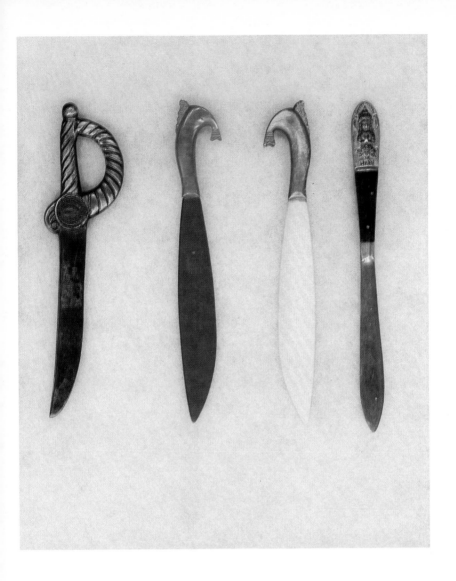

1: "State Capitol Richmond, VA" Knife Figural; aluminum w/ brass finish; 6 3/4" $10

2: "The Island of Lepers- San Antonio, TX"; plastic; 7" $5

3: "The Isle of Hope- San Antonio, TX"; plastic; 7" $5

4: "Siam" Idol Relief; bronze; 7" $10

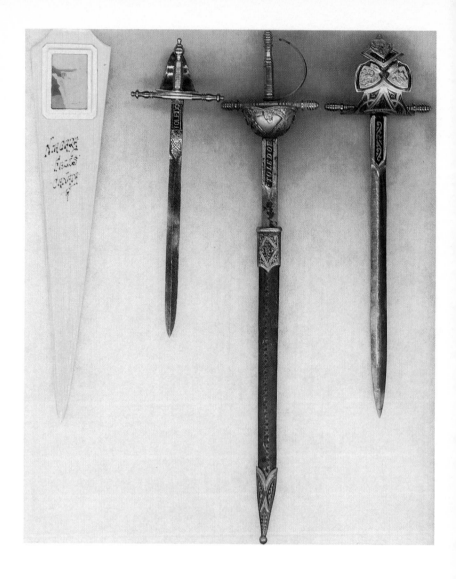

1: "Niagara Falls, Canada"; plastic-"French Ivory"; 8 3/8"; (Note: inset photo of Niagara Falls on framed end) $15

2: "Toledo" Sword Figural; metal; 6 1/2" $10

3: "Toledo: Sword Figural w/ Scabbard; metal; 9 1/4"; (Made in Spain) $20

4: "Spain" Sword Figural; metal; 8 1/4" $10

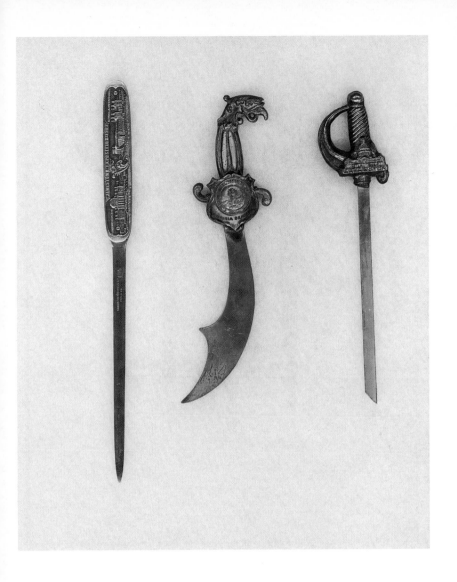

1: "Jamestown Exposition 1907"; pewter and steel; 8 1/2"; (Mfg: Magnetic Cutlery Co., Phila. PA) $30

2: "Virginia Beach, VA" Scimitar Figural; bronze; 6 1/2" $10

3: "Washington" Sword Figural; bronze w/ copper finish; 6 5/8" $10

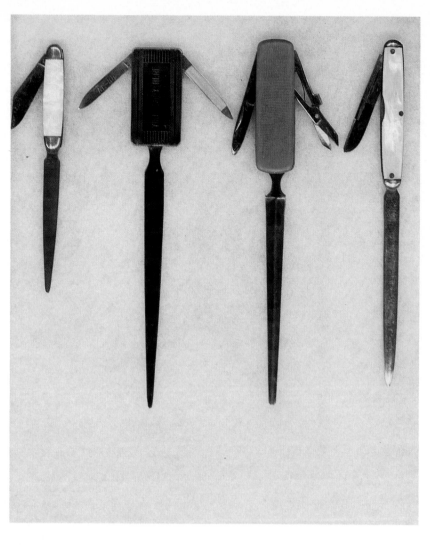

1: Opener/ Penknife Combination; metal w/ mother of pearl; 5 1/4";
(Mfg: Imperial USA) $10

2: Opener/ Penknife Combination; stainless steel; 7 1/2"; (Mfg:
Imperial USA); (Note: salesman's sample) $15

3: Opener/ Penknife Combination; plastic and stainless steel; 7 3/4";
(Made in Japan) $10

4: Opener/ Penknife Combination; plastic and stainless steel; 7 1/4" $10

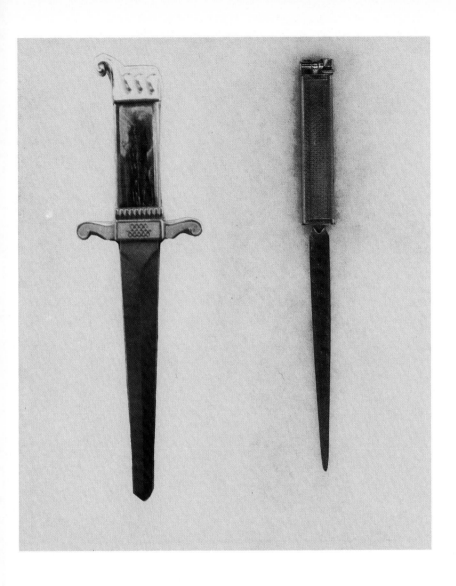

1: "ASR" Opener/ Lighter Combo; copper; 9 1/2"; (Made in Brooklyn, NY) $45

2: Dunhill "*Sylph*" Opener/ Lighter Combination; metal and gold plated metal; 8 3/4" $100

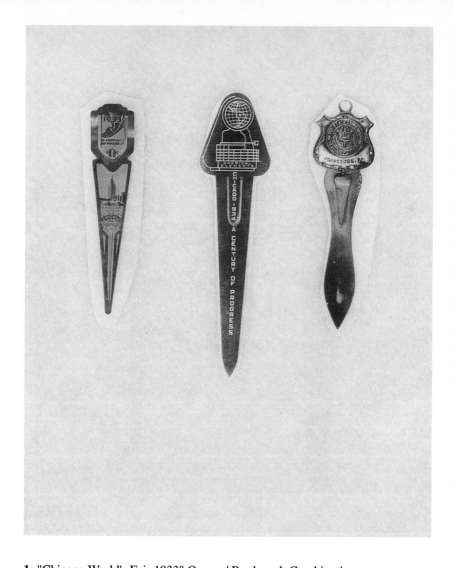

1: "Chicago World's Fair 1933" Opener/ Bookmark Combination; brass; 4 3/4" $25

2: "Chicago 1934 A Century of Progress" Opener/ Bookmark Combination; stainless steel; 6" $20

3: "State Seal of Pennsylvania - Johnstown, PA" Opener/ Bookmark Combination; stainless steel; 5" $10

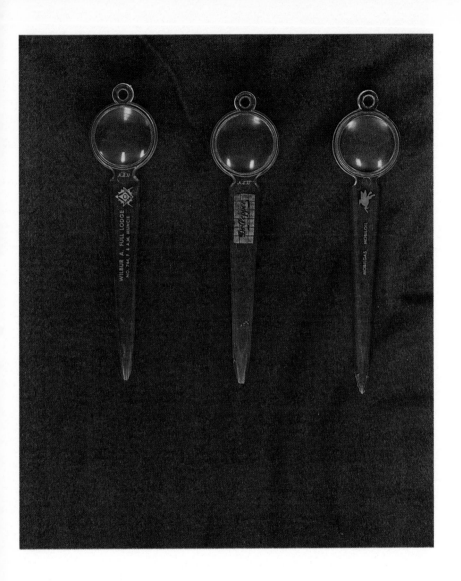

1: "Wilbur A. Full, Masonic Lodge" Opener/ Magnifying Glass
Combination; plastic; 6 1/4"; (Made in USA) $10

2: "Dr. Pepper" Opener/ Magnifying Glass Combination; plastic;
6 1/4"; (Made in USA) $10

3: "Mobil Gas - Mobil Oil" Opener/ Magnifying Glass Combination;
plastic; 6 1/4" $10

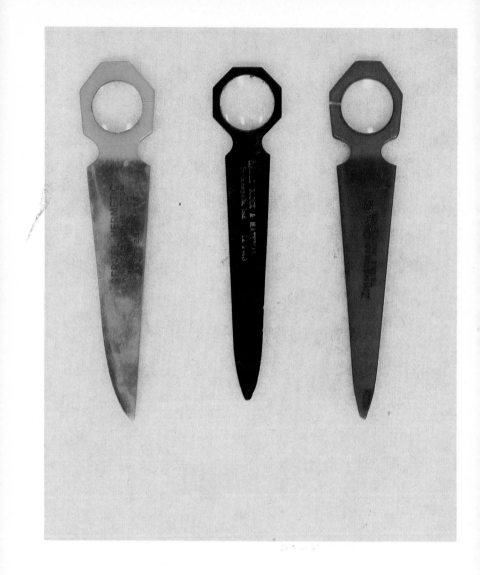

1: "Servel Hermetic Winners Convention 1931, Evansville, Ind." Opener/ Magnifying Glass/ Ruler Combination; plastic; 7 1/2" $15

2: "Cinder Block & Material Co., Indianapolis, Ind." Opener/ Magnifying Glass Combination; plastic; 7" $15

3: "Zimmerman Coal Co., Terre Haute, Ind." Opener/ Magnifying Glass/ Ruler Combination; plastic; 7 1/2"; (Made in Germany) $15

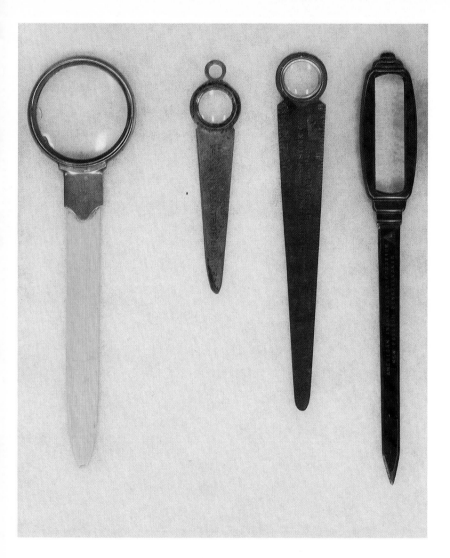

1: Opener/ Magnifying Glass Combination; metal and celluloid; 8 3/4";
(Made in Germany) $65
2: "Milk of Magnesia, Phospho-Muriate of Quinine" Opener/
Magnifying Glass Combination; nickel plated brass w/ glass; 4 7/8" $50
3: "Pennsylvania Paper Stock Co., Pittsburgh, PA" Opener/
Magnifying Glass Combination; bronze and glass; 7 1/2";
(Mfg: Whitehead & Hoag Co., Newark, NJ) $20
4: "American Insulator Corporation- ALCO, New Freedom, PA"
Opener/ Magnifying Glass Combination; bronze; 9"; (Mfg: K-D
Mfg. Co., Lancaster, PA) $30

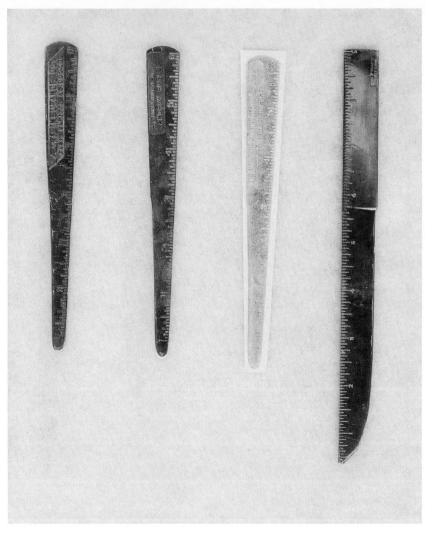

1: "Aetna Insurance Co." Opener/ Ruler Combination; aluminum; 6 1/2"; (ca. 1910) $5

2: "Compliments of Andrew Russel" Opener/ Ruler Combination; aluminum; 6 1/2"; (ca. 1910) $5

3: "Aluminum Cooking Utensil Co." Opener/ Ruler Combination; aluminum; 6 1/2"; (ca. 1910) $5

4: Opener/ Ruler Combination; stainless steel; 8 3/4"; (Made in Solingen, Germany); (Note: etching of city skyline on reverse side) $5

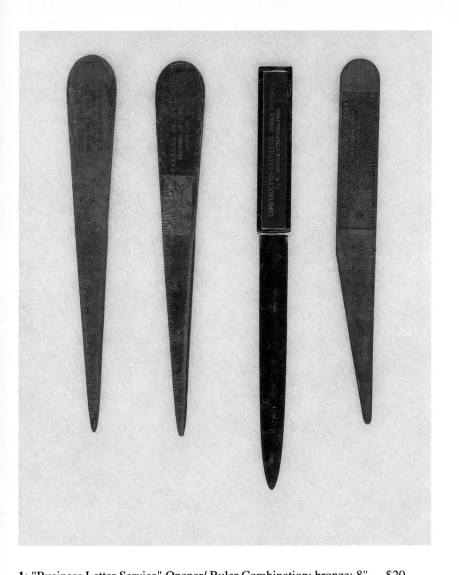

1: "Business Letter Service" Opener/ Ruler Combination; bronze; 8" $20

2: "College of Commerce- Newark, Ohio", bronze; 8" $20

3: "Construction Statistics- Dodge Reports" Opener/ Ruler
Combination; stainless steel; 8 7/8"; (Mfg: Latama "Italy") $10

4: "Geo. J. Mayer Co." Opener/ Ruler Combination; bronze; 7 3/4" $20

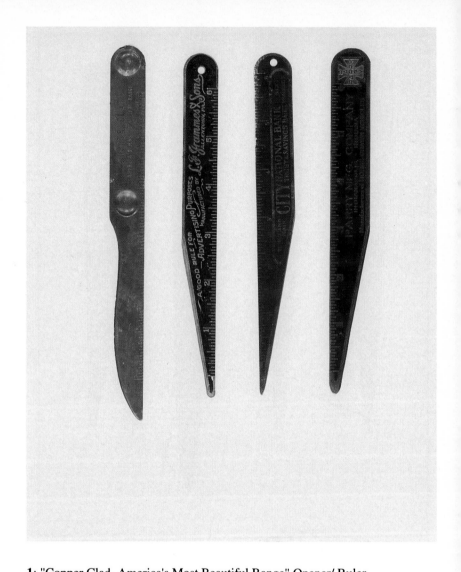

1: "Copper Clad- America's Most Beautiful Range" Opener/ Ruler
Combination; copper; 8"; (ca. 1923) $20

2: "L.F. Grammes & Sons- Allentown, PA"; Opener/ Ruler
Combination; bronze; 7 1/4"; (ca. 1915) $20

3: "City National Bank" Opener/ Ruler Combination; bronze; 7 1/4" $20

4: "Parry Mfg. Company- Indianapolis, Ind." Opener/ Ruler
Combination; copper; 7 1/4"; (ca. 1915) $20

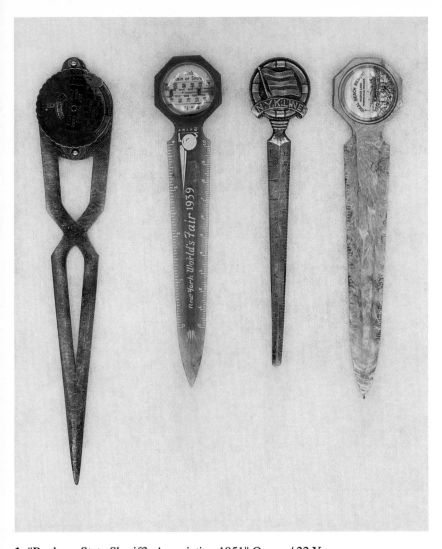

1: "Buckeye State Sheriff's Association 1951" Opener/ 22 Year
Calendar 1951-1972; metal; 9" $25

2: "New York World's Fair 1939" Opener/ Ruler/ Thermometer
 Combination; plastic; 7" $35

3: "N.Y.K. Line" Opener/ Ruler Combination; metal; 6" $35

4: "Ideal Beach Resort - Shafer Lake, Monticello, Ind"; plastic;
7 1/8" $5

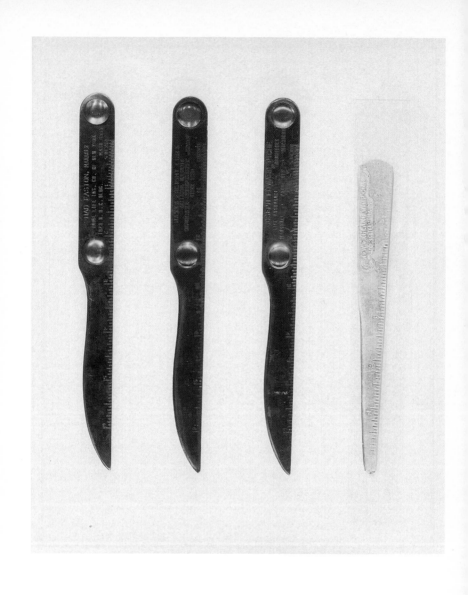

1-3: Opener/ Ruler Combinations; bronze; 7 7/8"; (Note: very common design among advertisers) $10each

4: "New England Whip Co.- Westfield, MA"; Opener/ Ruler Combination; aluminum; 6 1/2" $20

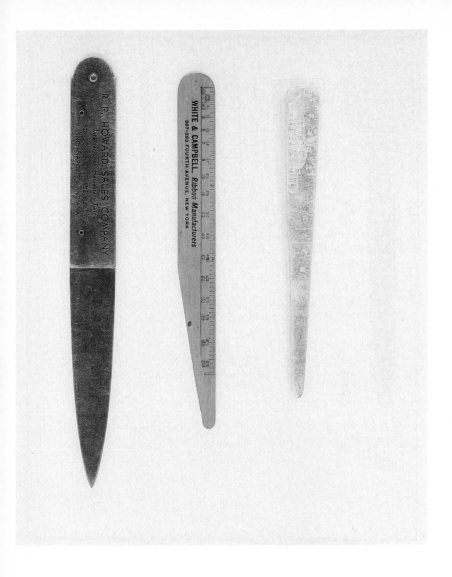

1: "R.R. Howard Sales Company- Indianapolis, Ind." Opener/ Ruler Combination; stainless steel; 9 1/4" $10

2: "White & Campbell Ribbon Manufacturers"; Opener/ Ruler Combination; wood; 7 1/2" $10

3: "Ohio State Fair- Columbus, Ohio" Opener/ Ruler Combination; aluminum; 6 1/2"; (ca. 1910) $20

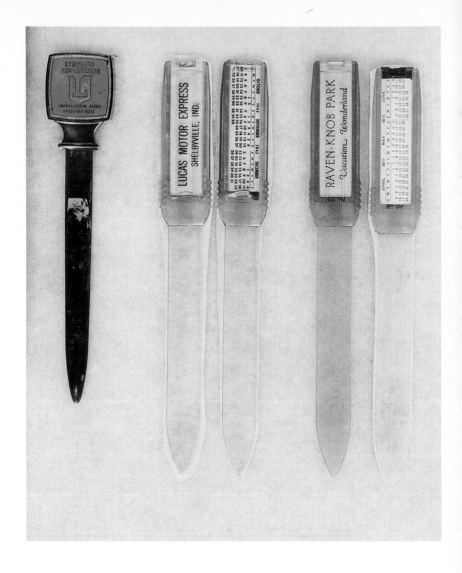

1: "Lynmark Advertising- Long Meadow, Mass." Opener/ Tape Measure Combination; stainless steel; 7 1/2" $15

2: "Lucas Motor Express- Shelbyville, Ind." Opener/ Calendar Combination; plastic; 8 3/4"; (ca. 1943) $20

3: "Raven Knob Park- Vacation Wonderland"; Opener/ Calendar Combination; plastic; 8 3/4"; (ca. 1949) $20

1: "Standard Compliments of Louis Getche" Opener/ Pen Combination; plastic; 7 3/4" $10

2: "Citizens National Bank of Paris, Ill." Opener/ Pen Combination; plastic; 7 1/2" $10

3: "Regency Hyatt House- Atlanta, Georgia"; Opener/ Level Combination; plastic; 7 1/4" $20

4: "Eskay- Meadow Gold" Opener/ Pen Combination; plastic; 7 5/8"; 1955 $10

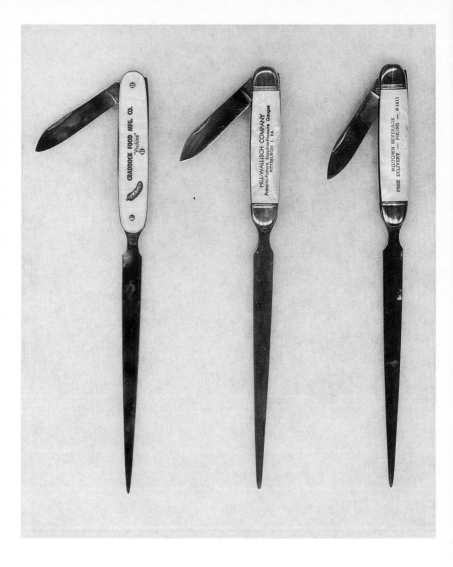

1: "Craddock Food Mfg. Co." Opener/ Penknife Combination; plastic and metal; 9" $30

2: "Hill-Wallisch Company- Pittsburgh, PA" Opener/ Penknife Combination; plastic and metal; 9" $30

3: "Midtown Beverage" Opener/ Penknife Combination; plastic and metal; 9" $30

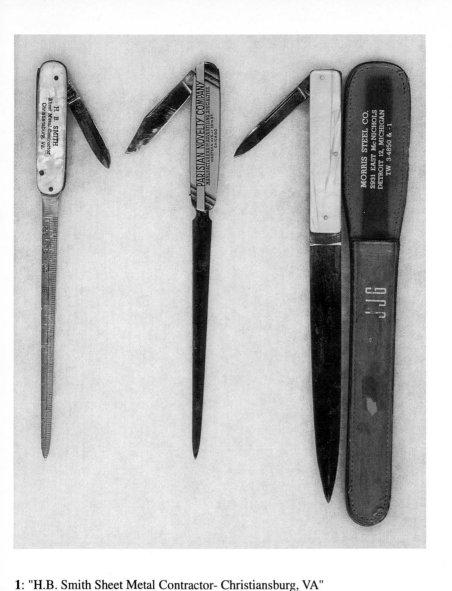

1: "H.B. Smith Sheet Metal Contractor- Christiansburg, VA"
Opener/ Penknife/ Ruler Combination; plastic and metal; 8 3/8" $20

2: "Parisian Novelty Company- Manufacturer of Advertising
Specialties" Opener/ Penknife Combination; metal; 8 3/8"; (ca. 1915) $35

3: "Morris Steel Co." Opener/ Penknife Combination; plastic and
metal; 9 1/4"; (Note: w/ monogrammed leather sheath) $30